you're completely normal

TRADING WHERE YOU THINK YOU SHOULD BE FOR WHERE YOU WANT TO GO

SHANNON LEYKO

ISBN: 978-0-578-74261-8

Cover photo by Melina Glover Photography
Design by Vanessa Mendozzi

For Anders and Jo

May your lives unfold with fervent intention
and joyous surprise.

For Aaron

I love drinking the good wine with you.

CONTENTS

CHAPTER 4: health & fitness

CHAPTER 5: parenthood

CHAPTER 6: friendships

CHAPTER 7: hobbies & service

CHAPTER 8: residence

CHAPTER 9: faith

INTRODUCTION

DON'T SAVE THE GOOD WINE

I was 24 when my mother died of bladder cancer. It was as sudden as it was inexplicable. She was a triathlete, registered nurse, and nature enthusiast with a lineage of strong women who enjoyed the occasional glass of inexpensive wine and lived well into their nineties. Yet I found myself at her bedside asking her to teach me one final lesson before she'd even had the chance to help me pick out a wedding dress, become a grandmother, or rent that little RV camper she always talked about for retirement.

This is what she said:

"Shannon, don't save the good wine. Downstairs, there are a few bottles of wine I was saving for a special occasion, and now I'll never know what they taste like."

I held her hand a few days later as she left this world, in awe of her peace and grateful for her imparted wisdom before we said goodbye. From that point forward, my life hinged on this single phrase:

Don't save the good wine.

This isn't about throwing all caution to the wind because "you only YOLO once," as my husband likes to say. (I married him for his Dad jokes.) And it isn't about my personal, very real friendship with wine—which I consider sacred, as it was the subject of Jesus' first miracle. No, my mom's sentiment holds a far more pressing message: You mustn't let what you think you *should* do dictate your ability to be happy *in the present.*

Dreaming of the future is one of my favorite parts of being alive, but this is a book about creating the foundation of daily contentment, gratitude, and confidence within your *current* stratosphere so that your soul has the energy to flourish. Then your dreams can truly take off. This is about drinking the wine today, not wishing you had back then or waiting until the time is just right.

Then and *when* aren't when you should do anything. Your life is a gift and a full-blown story as it exists this very second. As busted or boring as it might seem. Embrace it. Crack open the vino!

Your story is made up of days, and days are made up of all the little moments that meld into your singular, unrepeatable existence. Think of each facet of your life (health, family, career, etc.) as a coils of a spring, and their harmony creates a springboard for not only your grandiose purpose and dreams, but your day-in, day-out, unrelenting joy. Boing!

Relationships, pursuits, and beliefs that comprise our everyday existence all too often make us feel inferior in how they unfold. We feel like we're falling behind as each year of life runs parallel to yet another expected milestone. Thanks to generational teachings passed down by well-intentioned parents, educators, and [perhaps not so well-intentioned] media, we've grown up believing that our paths in life should all generally align with the person next to us.

You know how it goes…first comes love, then comes marriage…preferably before you turn 35, but not before 25 because then you're just wasting your youth.

Tell me if this sounds familiar: Take a few years in your early 20s to "find yourself" (i.e. show up to work hungover), but you should be squarely in your career of choice by your mid-20s. Around then, marry someone. What, like it's hard? Within two years of the wedding, give birth. Your children should be 2.5 years apart and wear matching Easter outfits every spring. Meanwhile, get yourself a hobby (bonus points for one that pertains to being in shape!) otherwise you're a workaholic or a mombot. If your kitchen doesn't have a large center island by the time your kids are in middle school, you definitely haven't hustled hard enough. White cabinets. Only white. Know exactly how you feel about politics and religion, and be able to defend those beliefs with educated eloquence, or else you're just an unenlightened talking head, brainwashed by CNN or Fox or Trish from Sunday School.

Shewww!

I seriously wonder how our goals and dreams are ever supposed to take flight when we're so bogged down by the constraints of what we *should* be doing. My dad is a pilot. I think a lot about airplane weight when I'm flying, and I know too much baggage when I see it. No way is joy getting off the ground when we're loaded up with such massive amounts preconceived failure.

While our past is an influential part of our story, forming lives full of satisfaction stems from our mindset in the present. We can't measure our lives up against what could've or should've been. Joy and purpose live within the *What can I do right now?* thought process. There's nothing like the self-fulfilling prophecy of snowballing our regrets by paralyzing ourselves over what we did or didn't do in the past. As if our soul is made merely for the purpose of being tethered to a narrow timeline.

There are a plethora of books out there that will motivate you to be the biggest, baddest version of yourself through pursuing your dreams and harnessing the power of your talent. I've read about seven trillion of them, and undoubtedly they're why this book is even in your hands. But something I've wrestled with in my own life is this nagging feeling that achieving my dreams won't really tackle the inner voice that says "You're not doing this right" and "You're not where you should be." It's why getting to the top leaves people so miserable—at least from what I've read about in *People*. When you arrive, you discover that "arrival" is just a figment of your imagination. It's not even real.

What if instead of waiting for the benefits of achieving a dream to trickle down into our daily lives, we meet ourselves where we are right this very second to develop a foolproof springboard to joy? What if you take each aspect—each spring coil—of your life that feels rusted or cumbersome, and polish it up? What if you shift your view of those lagging areas of life from "uniquely lonely and hopelessly delayed" to "completely normal and easily improved upon"?

Stifling our happiest, best selves is all too easy when we let things like our marital status, job title, or perpetual dishes in the sink define our Report Card of Life. Maturing is important, but morphing into a streamlined ghost of who you were created to be is a profoundly disturbing missed opportunity.

So, how do we throw out the inadequacy, and instead use where our life "should be" as motivation to strive for our own brand of greatness?

Each chapter of this book will explore an area of your life that is vulnerable to the idea that you're behind. Behind your peers, behind your childhood dreams, behind your parents' expectations. *Mom taught me to make the bed a million years ago and I still don't do it. I'm the worst. I will never reach maturity! When will I ever grow up?*

We're going to rewire that voice in your head—the super annoying one I just mocked—and tell it to relax with all the drama. It says that the ship has sailed, but it's wrong.

You will have a handle on some chapters in this book, and other chapters will be speaking right to you. No one's story is all smooth-sailing, because that would be a really lame story, so nod along with the parts that feel breezy to you, and hunker down with the parts that get a little choppy. I hope you'll find solace in knowing you aren't managing the waves alone.

CHAPTER 1

relationships

SPRAY TANS

As I write, I am currently seven months pregnant. There's a heating pad on my back and holes in my maternity leggings. My idea of dressing up is to slide on Uggs instead of fishing boots (the footwear of choice for my small town in Alaska) and pop in contact lenses in place of my scratched-up glasses. There's always the option to add a dab of under-eye concealer if I'm feeling particularly frisky! Forget shaving—I save my minimal bendability for putting on socks or occasionally picking up my toddler's mountain of toys so that I can carve a path to the couch.

Six years ago, I was a size 2, spray-tanned fan of mini skirts and manicures, living in New York City. In fact, I was Miss New York. You heard me correctly. We're talking a rhinestone crown on the red carpet with Mayor Bloomberg and fake eyelashes for tourist photo ops at the Freedom Tower. I was hugging babies at fundraisers, headlining at middle school assemblies, singing the national anthem for a few thousand people, and even making the occasional appearance on national news programs—the whole shebang.

Amidst the moments of glamour was my actual day job waitressing at an upscale Italian steak house in Times Square. Miss New York gigs didn't cover the bills, but that was alright. Are you even living in New York if you don't keep up the hustle?! I spent my free time relaxing in my 250 square foot studio apartment in Washington Heights, a neighborhood made famous by Lin Manuel Miranda but still barely makes the cut on most maps of Manhattan. I wasn't exactly Carrie Bradshaw or anything sexy and spectacular (I choose to ignore the blatant incongruence of her career and her apartment size), but I was living out pieces of my dream, even if it meant serving meatballs to Neil Patrick Harris and dealing with misogynistic coworkers. Carrie and I did have something in common besides our love for writing and living in the New York, however: We both found out that dating in the City is the actual worst, even for those of us who can throw on some charm and stilettos like a second skin.

You see, at the experienced and ripened age of 24, I was already behind schedule. I have always been a relationship person, and I was confident in my desire to be a wife. *Surely I should've found Mr. Right by now!*

Now, any reasonable person will tell you that New York City is not the place for a 24-year-old to find a monogamous, happy relationship. I'm not sure New York City is where you go to find love at any age, unless that love is a career or creativity or bagels and schmear. Nonetheless, I was in the market for Notebook-level romance, preferably with a brunette 6'0" or taller with a decent job, strong values, and an openness to one day getting married and having kids. Right. I was also on the hunt for a cow as white as milk, a cape as red as blood, the hair as yellow as corn, and a slipper as pure as gold. (For my musical theatre geeks: I once served Stephen Sondheim at my restaurant. Very exciting.)

My willingness to admit that I was ready to settle down under the age of 30 was enough for a few of my friends to recommend therapists and street-corner medication. They also suggested I learn to "love myself first" and "live while I was young," so I learned to ignore the annoyed look on their faces when I professed my want for a relationship because their buzzword platitudes were, in return, equally annoying.

Despite serving as a near-useless setting for my ultimate goal of love and marriage, New York *did* offer me a viable quest for a career in musical theatre—a path that everyone around me told me I should pursue, so I did. Besides, I thought that if anyone had a chance at an award-winning vocal career *and* love in the City, it was me.

Shooting for the impossible has never been my personal weak point.

Surely someone would think I'm take-back-home material. Tan legs, remember?? Size 2! Blue eyes and an outgoing personality! Rhinestones included. *Come one, come all! Fly me out to the Midwest to meet your family in the town you're so embarrassed to be from! Invite me to your boring banker holiday party! Let's drink whiskey at a low-key dive because I'm cool enough to do that!*

Can you smell the desperation? Even eight years removed, I'm still not sure the stench has completely left me. Or maybe that's the refried beans my toddler just spilled on my shirt. Awesome.

My point, unless I beguiled you with notions of tiaras and Wicked auditions, is to say that I, like many women, was once at a point in my life where the idea of love clenched my soul and led me down an exhausting path of passion, excitement, heartache, and too much self-tanner. I didn't understand why no one loved me in a stage of life where I felt that I was my most attractive, both physically and socially. (Turns out those things don't matter much—someone please inform the beauty industry.)

The words "your time will come" felt like a condescending blow to my ego, and worse, an overly confident cliché that only further stroked my biggest fear: *What if my time never comes? What if I'm one of those women who wakes up at age 65 and never found someone to share her life with? And now it's time to retire—and what then—I wait around until I die alone??*

You might be able to gather why the dramatic arts was a good fit for my personality.

Still, I was right. You cannot guarantee a single person that she will end up in a happy, healthy relationship before she turns the age where her ovaries shut down and the skin on her neck resembles an accordion folder. It is this truth that ate me alive.

But you know what, you guys? The odds are really freakin' good that you'll end up with someone. As of 2014, the Social Security Administration says that 95% of the American population age 65 years and older has been married at least once. (I don't know if the "at least once" part is encouraging or depressing, but we'll go with encouraging for our purposes.)

What you must cling to, and what you must understand, is that falling in love, planning your dream wedding, and one day sitting next to your spouse in holey maternity leggings paired with spiky armpits has *nothing* to do with a projected timeline or fancy heels. I say that from experience. Making comparisons to other people and relationships will do absolutely NOTHING to expedite the process, and "looking attractive" only goes so far in actually landing and maintaining a thriving relationship. And by "so far," I mean about the length of those rolled Soffe shorts you used to lure in the boys when you hit puberty.

This ideal of falling in love is not found on a train roaring past us, each subway car flying by like a missed opportunity. We can't expect this imaginary train to stop and pick us up just because we have on a cute beret and the perfect plaid pea coat like we're some kind of magnificent 1950s English starlet. Love isn't even on the train to begin with, so stop waiting on the platform! There is no train!

True Love plucks you out of oblivion like a needle from a haystack, usually when you have on yesterday's mascara. Of course there are ways to make yourself a bit more available (I'm sorry, but True Love will not magically burst through your DMs— unless you're the girl who's engaged to Ben Higgins), but no app or devotion to Drybar can guarantee you a healthy, lifelong relationship by the age of 30. Or in my sad little hopeful case, age 24. You must wait until it's your time to be plucked from the haystack. (And I remember how scratchy that hay can feel as you wait. Woof.)

Instead of searching and fretting or regretting, take a dive with me into some legitimate truths about how relationships *really* look in our modern world, without the filters and catch-phrases created by society that only make you feel more alone. #selflove

YOU ARE NOT AN ALLIGATOR

Single ladies, gather round. It's time for an honest chat. [Sips wine.]

I know Beyoncé makes you feel like a queen because you run the world, and you don't need a man to do so. I know that it's sweet to call your girlfriends your soulmates because that's what a writer on *Sex and the City* came up with. I am fully aware of the stigma that comes with admitting you'd rather be in a relationship than go through life unattached. After all, us modern ladies all know that happiness doesn't come from another person. That the only person you can rely on is yourself. That if you don't love yourself first, then you're incapable of loving anyone else. Yada yada yada.

I could go on and on listing off all the catchphrases and song lyrics and flowery quotes associated with singlehood. And while many of these notions are more true than false, they're mainly just a whole bunch of shameballs rolling toward women. *Apparently* women aren't strong enough to figure out our own wants and needs without society assigning us coffee mug phrases to live by. Judging by how often men quote whimsical language about their relationship status (hint: never), they don't need constant reminders that they're fine without a significant other. By throwing shameball catchphrases at women, society is constantly using romance to encompass our identities, while simultaneously admonishing us for thinking about it too much. They've decided we need help. And wordy kitchen towels.

Men and women alike grapple with wanting a relationship but not wanting to look weak by desiring companionship. It's the plight of the entire 21st century—this push for complete independence as if we're reptilian, not communal mammals. I know a lot about reptiles because my son loves *Gator Boys*, and let me tell you something: I do not function like an alligator. Alligators are lone rangers without feelings or social attachment. Survival is their only mission. They lack any primal need for the presence of fellow life forms other than those they eat.

So why does modern self-help sound more and more like a description of scaly carnivores?

You don't have to look far to figure out where this narrative of desiring companionship making someone weak comes from—especially for women. I'm sure it relates to the history of women being stifled by men, made unequal outside of the home and entirely responsible inside of the home, therefore weakening their ability to pursue dreams and gifts beyond homemaking. Flipping outdated roles on their heads means we've reassigned weakness to anything that remotely resembles yesteryear. The classic pendulum swing.

I'm sure it also relates to the fall of valuable, tangible

community that has been replaced by social media friendships and swiping right. Not to mention the relatively recent ability to travel wherever we please, get in touch with whomever we please, and do whatever makes us feel good in the moment, be it order pizza to our doorstep or fire off a drunk text to our ex. In a world (well, country) of immediate gratification and endless choices, we unsurprisingly begin to feel like our dependence on another human for survival is less necessary. And for basic alligator-type survival, it *is* less necessary.

However, in case you need to hear it in plain words: You are not an alligator. We're not aiming for basic survival here. We're in the market for meeting the needs and desires of our souls. Somehow the message of being able to take care of ourselves has merged with the idea that you should no longer show interest in finding a committed, romantic partnership.

That's quite a leap.

Can we please step back and recognize the absurdity of it? Why are we putting pressure on ourselves to stifle an age-old desire and natural phenomenon? Human beings have been falling in love with each other since the beginning of time. Adam and Eve, Jacob and Rachel, Cleopatra and Mark Antony, Johnny and June, Justin and Britney, Nick and Jessica, Ellen and Portia, Barack and Michelle.

If you want to point out that all of my teenage couple-idols didn't end up together, I'm going to need you to let me live.

The opposing—or perhaps tandem—theories that love is either biological *or* a cultural phenomenon have been assessed and interpreted for years. Why pick a side? Biology and culture *both* play into our hope to find a life partner—even confusing modern culture that tells us it's unnecessary to fall in love, but then releases movies like *The Notebook* or *Sweet Home Alabama* as if we're not going dream about Ryan Gosling or Josh Lucas upending their lives for us. (Please take me back to the early 2000s.)

In an article for *Time*, psychologist Lawrence Casler concluded that love is a result of societal pressure (not human nature). Author Kendra Cherry held this idea up against research by anthropologist Helen Fisher, who studied and identified romantic love in 147 of 166 societies.

Cherry wrote, "[Fisher's] study, along with countless others, suggests that there is a biological component to love—a part of human nature that seeks out and finds love. Likewise, because Fisher could not identify romantic love in every society she studied, this suggests that there is a cultural influence to love as well."

See? Both!

If your little heart is yearning for a mate, it's not only vital to your self-esteem and self-acceptance that you don't feel ashamed of that desire, but I want you to acknowledge that it's completely natural to feel that way! We have a biological need for belonging, reproduction, and intimacy, as well as a culture brewing with undertones that contradict the inspirational quote memes on Instagram.

If you think you'd be happier with someone to share your meals with, to provide physical affection, to converse with about your day, to parent alongside, to come home to every night—then you know what? That's part of your spirit's makeup! It's not a silly, weak, old-fashioned pining that you need to hide, suppress, or squash. New schools of thought are not always better, particularly when they're imposed on us rather than sparked from our own internal compass.

Lean into your truth! If your *truth* is that you prefer to be alone and genuinely don't desire a relationship, that's cool, too. I mean it. It just seems to me, however, that a lot more people are trying to convince themselves that they're that person than existing in that headspace naturally or comfortably.

To really hammer this home, I'm going to be honest with you and say some things I'm not supposed to say:

I prefer being married to being single.

I'm generally happier day in and day out than I was when I was single.

I rely on my husband for emotional, physical, and spiritual strength.

I would take the stressful moments in marriage over the stressful moments in solitude.

I feel more complete, content, and fulfilled now that I am sharing my life with another individual.

Dang, I'm really doing a great job making my single or unhappily married friends feel a lot better, aren't I? But stay with me! I've got you! I needed to start with squashing the whole *independence rules* attitude, otherwise nothing else I write will matter. I want you to be confident in admitting and expressing your relational desires, just as I'm confident admitting and expressing that 24-year-old me was right, after all. I desired marriage because I knew it would significantly add to my happiness. And it does.

This discrepancy in what we tell the world (and ourselves) we want—i.e. suiting up for emotional autonomy—and what we *really* want can be seen in nearly every poll and survey taken by reputable data banks in the last 10 years. Gallup polls, Pew Research Center, and even a survey conducted by trusty *Vanity Fair* all show that the majority of never-married singles in the United States desire to one day marry. I went in deep on this research. You're welcome.

Interestingly enough, though, Pew Research found that 39% of Americans believe marriage is obsolete...and yet, only 14% said they *don't* desire marriage. In 2013, Gallup found that percentage to be even lower among millennials, at only 9% of never-marrieds saying they don't desire marriage. If nearly 40% of people claim marriage is pointless, but 91% still want to get married someday (or at least don't know for sure either way)...then what this data shows is that we all need to be a little more honest with ourselves, yes?

I can infer the conflicted state of hearts in this world not only from these polls, but also from listening to more than half my friends lament the idea of marriage until they found the person they actually wanted to marry. I can't tell you how many times I heard "I just don't know if I even believe in marriage," then watched that same person say "I do" a year later after falling in love with a worthy partner.

In the timeless display of emotional self-preservation, our sensitive species definitely likes to poo-poo any institution that makes us feel insecure or unwanted, using the age-old defense mechanism of "Well I don't like you, either!" This is a much more gratifying deduction than coming to terms with the fact that we want in on the action. It reminds me of the wedding resale website neverlikeditanyway.com. We all have the proclivity for a little spite, am I right?

One of the most painful parts of not being in a relationship when that's something you openly or not-so-openly desire is the feeling of implied rejection. *Why has no one chosen me? What am I lacking?* We begin looking for a blameworthy cause, which usually lands on our own shoulders. Sure, occasionally we'll vent to our friends about the horrific dating pool full of noncommittal, immature playboys, or we might point fingers at poor parental example, personal trauma, or chalk it all up to bad luck. But most of us? Most of us fear the worst—that it's our own fault one of the "good ones" has yet to scoop us up. That we'll never be able to lock it down because we're not pretty enough, funny enough, successful enough, popular enough…enough enough enough. We tell ourselves that we're just not enough.

In our 20s, my single friends and I masked our frustrations and insecurities with humor. One of my friends was convinced that a troll lived in her lady parts, another thought she was doomed because she didn't like to wear bright colors, and I was the girl who was sure I had a chip missing—the one that makes people lovable.

I imagined the shape and size of this love chip. It was gold and looked exactly like those SIM cards in your smart phones. When creating me, God was supposed to insert it somewhere between my frontal lobe and parietal lobe, but He ultimately decided I could live without it.

This omission was not a mistake. God does not make mistakes. He purposefully excluded this chip so that I would become an independent spinster who could channel all of her energy into writing books about some unidentified important subject that would inspire the masses. God knew I would learn to be okay with this, mostly because I'd have no other choice.

Almost every relationship I entered ended with the guy saying, "I think you're wonderful and here are all the reasons why you're the greatest, but something is missing." The red flag during these conversations was the laundry list of all of the reasons these guys said they "should" want to be with me, but didn't.

Obviously, I was trying too hard to compensate for the missing chip, so bachelors never saw my raw self, and therefore could not pinpoint the reason why they were ending things. (Turns out people can usually sense when you're not being authentic. Bummer for 25-year-old me.) However, I should have known that any behavioral efforts to be more lovable would be futile. After all, no amount of determination can replace a love chip. Give it up. Since the men were so perplexed about the breakups, themselves, the only closure I ever received was self-acknowledgment of this missing chip.

When my husband, Aaron, told me that he loved me only two months after meeting each other, and two weeks after he first called me his girlfriend, I thought he was confused. This was partly because it accidentally slipped out when he was telling a random story over Mexican food, and partly because of my love chip predicament. With Aaron, I had not behaved in a way I thought to be ideal. By that point in my life (a geriatric 27) I knew things would not work out in the long run—how else would I end up alone? Therefore, I gave in to my imperfect ways. I didn't shave my legs every day, I openly admitted to him that my friends and I stalked pictures of his ex-girlfriend on Facebook, and I told him that sometimes his wardrobe choices come across like perhaps he's not into women.

These are not tactics I would suggest to anyone looking to nail down a solid [hetero] relationship.

Yet, here we are.

One and half kids later (two by the time you read this), I've come to realize that it was never about a chip. *Ya think, Shannon??* It was about breaking the facade of being a "chill" girl who didn't scare someone off with my dream-big tendencies or hermit preferences. My God, I am so glad I will never again partake in a St. Patrick's Day bar crawl just because the dude I'm dating thinks *it's such a good time, bro*. I'm not a proponent of turning into a Stage 5 Clinger or becoming codependent, but if a guy you've been exclusively dating for two months gets testy just because you casually mention his upcoming birthday, RUN. Before he does.

The desire I had for a companion isn't something that should've made me insecure. Nothing was wrong with me for wanting something that had not yet found its way into my life. The fact that I let it erode me into a shell of myself to appease men who clearly would never connect with my soul not only diminished my self-worth, but ironically created a self-fulfilling prophecy. Even if there was a decent guy among the motley crew I dated, how could he ever know and love me if I refused to be honest about who I was and what I wanted? It reminds me of my favorite poem, "Masks" by Shel Silverstein. I'd love to include it here, but copyright is a thing and your girl can't afford to take on a juggernaut like Shelly boy. Go ahead—Google it on your phone real fast. *She had blue skin and so did he…* basically, if you're both trying to hide your blue, you'll never find the person who makes you feel most understood. (Trust me, the short poem is far better than my synopsis.)

We all want our blue person! So we must be brave enough to show our blue!

I deeply believe the most critical component in finding your person is owning your authenticity by admitting to yourself that a relationship is, in fact, important to you.

Now, confidence is different than desperation. Confidence leads to furthering your authenticity by valuing self-improvement and expending energy in other areas of your life that bring you joy or build upon your talents. Desperation is a one-track mind, suffocating the beauty of life found outside of a romantic relationship and therefore presenting a hollow, unappealing version of yourself that won't get you anywhere.

Finding confidence in your biological and cultural desire for companionship not only allows you to feel less crazy and more sincere, but it lets your insecurities off the hook. Your personality, your body, your quirks, your flaws—those things are not to be blamed for your singlehood. The person you are is perfectly desirable—loud voice, unshaven legs and all. I am confident that I was not my "most desirable" when dating Aaron, but in those crevasses, my true light was able to shine and be loved.

So please know this, my single ladies or friends in need of a relationship overhaul: The natural desire for companionship must be met with total transparency. Be honest with yourself and the world about the kind of relationship you desire. Recognize that you are not in total control, thus giving yourself the permission to be boldly authentic so your fellow blue person doesn't pass you by.

Transparency about your relational desires lifts the heavy cloak on your shoulders that tries to hide the yearnings of your heart in the name of self-defense or popular opinion. Confidently admitting "I would prefer to share my life with someone else" is a far surer way to free yourself into a life you love than painfully building up a wall of independence that only comes natural to crocodilian.

Freedom in your wiring is always better.

Truth is always lighter.

THE PERKS OF BEING SINGLE

My 20s were challenging, growth-filled, and doused in outrageous, embarrassing, and poignant moments. When I was single, I often felt a wave of self-love and exuberant authority when I was squished between strangers on a crowded subway or when I drove on the highway with the windows down. In unexpected moments, I'd rediscover the power in my solitude and the freedom in my steps. To be without restriction to travel, save, spend, pray, learn, question, and sleep. (Bring me back to the sleep!)

Each moment of tuned-in idiosyncrasy laid an indestructible brick of conviction on the foundation of who I am. When I met Aaron, I didn't *want* to be by myself at that point in my life, but at least I knew what kind of person I was on my own: funny, loyal, moody, financially wise, and addicted to chunky peanut butter.

Clearly, being single can be *awesome*. While I want you to see that wanting a relationship doesn't make you weak or "unhappy with yourself," I also want you to fully digest what I said about control…in that you don't have all of it. In fact, you don't have most of it. So why waste your single years in a state of wishful thinking and being hard on yourself? I know many of you are much better than I was at embracing the single life and trusting that "your time will come." (Maybe you don't even want it to, for real.) Still, I know I'm not alone in having overlooked the benefits of being single when I was so.

It was in my single days that I learned how unreasonable I am when I haven't eaten, how susceptible I am to being led by heightened emotions, and how dangerously fast I give my heart to other people. It was then that I learned how to enjoy just one glass of wine, an entire box of cheesy bread, and even the act of occasionally going to the gym. [Pats self on back.] Before we parted ways, singlehood bestowed upon me lifelong, fulfilling friendships and the memories that came with them. It solidified the delight I feel in my family's presence, the need for God in my soul, and the passions I want to pursue.

Being single is more than a waiting game. It's more than being happy, free, confused and lonely at the same time. Uh, uh. Uh, uh… (If you weren't singing that with me, were you even alive in 2012?) Singlehood is a tremendous gift in its own right, laying a firm foundation for your future and yourself. It may last one year past 18, or it may last 30, but each moment you are without a partner is one worthy of respect, praise, and joy, because you, my dear, are becoming a formidable force.

FINDING YOUR PERSON

As you'll recall—at least, I hope so since it was just a few pages ago—the timeline of my love story didn't exactly line up with what I hoped for when I was younger. I still got married relatively early in life, but that was simply because Aaron and I got engaged in less time than contestants do on *The Bachelor*.

More on that later.

Like me, most of us have an arbitrary age in our head that signifies the turning point in our lives for when we'd like to be boo'd up. I'll be talking about marriage throughout this book, but feel free to replace that institution with whatever type of relationship you personally associate with #goals and use whatever pronoun makes sense in your universe.

You might be like my girlfriends who wanted nothing to do with a serious relationship or—God forbid—marriage, before they were 30. I mean, I would've had a heart attack, personally, if God had made me wait that long for a spouse since every bone I was born with ached for a relationship since I was approximately six years old and stalked a kid named Kyle in the first grade. So perhaps you're more like I am: strung out about falling in love since the moment you learned that was a thing.

Whatever that turning point age is for you—24, 30, or 45—it becomes more and more daunting as you near it without any prospects. Sometimes it starts creeping up while you are in a solid relationship, but that relationship doesn't seem to be moving forward anytime soon. *Can someone get the bling bling on the fing fing already?*

I was personally pretty worked up about my future by age 25 because not only had I already passed my turning point, but I noticed that most couples these days date for years and years before they get hitched. The math in my head went like this:

If I meet someone now, I still won't be engaged until I'm 27 at the earliest, married when I'm 28, then I want at least two years of being married before I have kids, which means no kids until I'm 30. And my eggs start declining in my early 30s, so that would be cutting it close if I want multiple kids. This is all if I meet the love of my life TOMORROW.

The sirens began to sound, the wine began to pour, and the panic fully set in. *I can*not *be responsible for killing cockroaches by myself my entire life. I just can*not*!*

It's true that modern couples date for an average of nearly five years—FIVE YEARS!—before marrying, according to a recent survey of 4,000 married couples. What the actual what? I mean, I get that you want to be totally sure, but five years? Y'all need to be better decision-makers than that, if you ask me. Experts say you should date for two years to fully know a person well enough to determine if they're well suited for an entire lifetime of happiness with you. I can get on board with that. But *five??*

Then there are the wackadoos like me who get engaged after two months of dating.

Before Aaron fell into my lap, I'd had my heart seriously broken three times, partly broken two other times, two breakups that didn't really break my heart at all, and a fling with a guy who went on to date pop star Camila Cabello. It's fine. I'm fine. Mixed in were approximately 1.7 million fledgling relationships that faltered after a week, a month, or the request for me to consider converting to Mormonism. He was *so* nice though.

Needless to say, I cast a wide net.

I was almost 27, and my dad convinced me to drive down from the DC area (where I was living at the time) for the weekend to casually discuss my hopes of moving to a new city. He'd suggested this little weekend after a particularly tearful phone call lamenting my job and DC's stuffy social scene and my roommate's affinity for group parties, so "Dad I'm just going to quit everything and move to Nashville!"

I never claimed to be an easy child.

Upon my arrival in Virginia Beach, Dad told me he'd found a potential apartment for me to lease about five minutes from his house, plus a job lead. "Dad, no way, I'm not moving back to my hometown this early in life. I need to move somewhere cool! Like Nashville, or San Diego!" Joke's on me, because my dad clearly knew I'd be easily swayed by the beachside one-bedroom once I laid eyes on the place. Bada bing bada boom—I signed the dotted line for a lease beginning in two months.

Touché, Father.

I wanted to celebrate this fly-by-the-seat-of-my-pants decision to suddenly up and move my life, so I texted some girlfriends I knew in Virginia Beach. They invited me to a house party happening that evening, and even though the introverted extrovert in me almost backed out at the last minute, I went.

It was April 25th. All I needed was a light jacket! (The pageant girl in me was thrilled at this coincidence after the fact.)

Unbeknownst to me, one of my friends invited a guy she thought might like to meet me. Sneaky little matchmaker. His name was Aaron. Despite hitting it off that night, he and I decided not to keep in contact while I was closing up shop in my old life. Remember—I was just in town for the weekend at this point.

A month later, I officially moved back to Virginia Beach, which he saw on Facebook (I don't think I even told him directly) and subsequently asked me out for a glass of wine the second night I was in town.

We were engaged two months later.

Trust me, I'm well aware this whole scenario was risky. He easily could've been a serial killer. The vast majority of my friends actually thought I was joking about the engagement until they came to their senses and realized it was me we were talking about, and if anyone was going to get engaged after two months, I'm your girl.

I can only imagine the things that were said in hushed phone calls—not out of cattiness, but out of concern and a bit of humor. Those who outright questioned my decision, or who I knew were quietly scrutinizing it among themselves, never offended me. I consider myself lucky to have friends who care enough about my happiness to raise a red flag when I say I'm going to spend the rest of my life with a guy whose middle name was still a question mark. (Just kidding, I knew it was Brandon. I mean Benjamin. It definitely starts with a B.)

Here's the big picture: Timelines are hardly in our control. In April of 2015, I was sure I'd die alone, unsatisfied in my job, and unhappy with my living situation. By December of the same year, I was married, happily settled in a beachside apartment in a new city, and about to quit my second job of the year in order to focus on my writing.

You see, things don't work out until *they do*.

Your life is always in the works of setting you up if you're willing to follow its lead. I promise, you'll never *not* be astonished at the magical puzzle pieces that had to perfectly align in order for your path to cross with Your Person. And it doesn't just begin the day you meet.

When I was 22, I went on a dog sledding trip in Ely, Minnesota with nine strangers because I'm a bit wild like that. A few weeks before I left, fresh off a painful and serious breakup, I went on a date after reluctantly giving my number to a slightly inebriated but good-looking dude at a random karaoke bar on Christmas night. What can I say? My rendition of Mariah Carey's "All

I Want for Christmas Is You" brings all the boys to the yard.

Mr. Christmas and I—shall we call him St. Nick?—went on three or four dates before I left on my big dog sledding adventure. I was pretty standoffish because I wasn't over the D-bag ice hockey player from college, but Nick was very attentive, so I leaned into the distraction.

And then I went off the grid for eight days. We're talking deep in the heart of No Man's Land, 10 miles south of the Canadian border during the brutal month of January in Minnesota, *dontcha know*. No shower for seven days. Definitely no shaving. All of the smells. By the time the trip was over, I was retaining at least 10 pounds of water weight due to all the special food we had to eat in order to stay warm in -15 degrees. My mother legitimately asked what happened to my face when she saw me.

Anyway, when I was sitting in the Minneapolis airport waiting to fly back home to Virginia, resembling Hagrid the groundskeeper after my somewhat harrowing but definitely enlightening expedition, I looked to my right and saw him. *Him*. Saint-freaking-Nick!

My immediate reaction: *RED ALERT. STALKER. Abort! Abort!*

At the exact same moment that I realized I may not want Nick to see me in my natural wildebeest condition and oversized college sweats, I heard a word escape from my mouth. *No no no no no Word, get back here!*

"Hey!"

Nick looked up at me, blinked a few times, cocked his head, and said, "...Shannon?"

I think he actually squinted. Nice.

Looking dapper in his tailored suit, he set down his iPad and gave me a big hug.

"What are you doing here??" he asked.

"Well, as you know because you took me to dinner the night before I left, I just finished my dog sledding trip about 40 miles north. So the real question is, what are YOU doing here?"

"I had a work conference in Arizona, and this is my layover on my way back home."

What are the odds.

Being the forward, romantic guy he was, Nick charmed a lady into switching seats with him, and I proceeded to pass out on his shoulder—slobber and all—the entire way back to Virginia. I must have some really strong pheromones to counteract the BO, because we ended up dating for three full months. Remember how long it took me to get engaged? Yeah. Three months is legit in my book. (Hey, this *is* my book!)

Even more amazing is that five years later, long after Nick realized he could never be with someone who doesn't deeply appreciate 80s music like he does, he wound up being the link between my husband and me. Remember when I moved back to Virginia Beach on a whim? The only friends I still knew in my hometown were those I'd met through Nick. One of them set me up with Aaron, and here we are. Nick and his wife even attended our wedding. Weird, but convenient.

If I hadn't drawn attention to myself with a pop sensation at a karaoke bar on Christmas night (what was my life?), or started dating this guy because an unlikely plane ride bonded us, I never would have met his friends, who became my friends, who then introduced me to my husband five years later.

Let your life do the work for you, because I promise—it is.

Sometimes, though, you've got to shake things up. Sing karaoke on Christmas night. Go on a dog sledding trip. Move to New York City. Then move again. And again. Those are some pretty bold choices, guys.

Far too often we are walking on a treadmill, wondering why our surroundings aren't changing. In order for life to work its magic, you've got to stir up some legitimate motion! It doesn't mean quitting your job on a whim and moving to a new city like I did. (Though I'm personally a big believer in relocation—it's not so hard, I promise!) How about simply picking up an old hobby?

Two months before I moved back to my hometown, I started taking horseback riding lessons again—my childhood love. Was I 15 years older than the other students? Sure was. But I tell you what, riding horses with high schoolers reminded me of the Good Life. It was in that headspace that I knew I could and should shake things up to be happy. It's probably why I had the gumption to sign that random lease in Virginia Beach.

Maybe hanging out with 14-year-olds and ponies isn't your thing. Maybe you're not even sure you have an old hobby. (Chapter 6 is for you, my friend!) How about this: Go out to drinks with a coworker instead of with the same crew of people you see every weekend. You'll meet new people, explore new spots, and develop new perspectives that your trusty crew doesn’t incite.

We value comfort, but comfort and growth aren’t found on the same end of the mountain. I’ll let you guess which one’s at the bottom and which one’s at the top.

THE GOLD RUSH

I like new places. I think that's been established. However, my affinity for a change of scenery has a couple of cons when it comes to meeting your match.

In 1932, sociologists at U Penn studied 5,000 married couples in Pennsylvania. He found that 40% of spouses lived within 20 blocks of each other when they met. Twenty blocks! That's your own neighborhood or the next one over. Twelve percent lived in the *same* apartment building! No need to even change your permanent address once you're carried across the threshold!

Aziz Ansari and sociologist Eric Klinenberg dove into some of the implications for the change in how and where modern singles meet one another in their book *Modern Romance*. Much of the shift has to do with the fact that for women, marriage used to be a form of freedom from parental control. I'm simplifying this, of course, but women weren't looking for Mr. Right—they were looking for Mr. Get Me Out of My Parents' House. With the bar set right around the height of my firstborn's balance beam at tot gym, it wasn't all that hard for women to find a match. Men weren't looking for an Insta model with a degree from Harvard, either. They just needed someone to cook and keep the house clean. [Insert eye roll.]

Now, that all probably sounds a bit icky to most of us, but if we're wondering why it's harder and harder to find a spouse than it was in "the good ole days," welp—consider the bar. Our generation wants to strike gold. The reason we believe we can is because we have access to boys and girls outside of the cul-de-sac. In fact, we have access to literally everybody.

Dating apps account for over a quarter of modern relationships. The choices are endless, and if you somehow *do* find an end, just move to a new city! Your app will reload and give you the next few hundred thousand eligible bachelors (and bachelorettes!) waiting to have an awkward drink with you.

Given that women are no longer dependent on a husband to fly the coop, men are generally comfortable pouring their own water these days (*generally*), and everyone everywhere has access to one another...well, why *not* raise the bar for our life partner?

As we've been liberated from the necessity of marriage and instead classify it as a preference, the courting process has slowed down for most of us. In many cases, it's even set our decision-making abilities on fire and triggered commitment-phobia. We will only accept "can't eat, can't sleep, reach for the stars over the fence world series kind of love," so if we lose that feeling a few years into the relationship or marriage, we cut our losses and move on.

When you raise the bar, it certainly complicates things. I

promise you are not less lovable than your great-grandmother.

On the plus side, in requiring more from our spouse than an exchange of skills, we have undoubtedly increased the probability that we'll find a true soulmate with deep compatibility and aligned lifestyles. If you don't buy a lottery ticket, you can't win, right? We're putting in the time, testing out the options, and kissing some frogs because we'd prefer to get it right than to spend our days making meatloaf for a man in oversized khakis.

My meatloaf is bomb, though, if I do say so myself.

So as we've increased our odds of finding Mr. Right by raising our standards, we've simultaneously decreased the probability that we'll find someone who we *want* to spend the rest of our lives with—especially not within some designated time frame. It's a gift and a curse, but either way, it is a cultural shift. We now have the freedom to connect with someone emotionally, intellectually, physically, and spiritually! But if you want to strike gold, you've got to spend some time digging.

THE PART YOU CAN CONTROL

In case you missed it, I really despise modern adages for singles like "focus on yourself" and "build your own life so you don't need another person to be happy." Sure, there's a nugget of truth in them, but they're mostly a narrow prescription to a widely individualistic stirring.

Instead of focusing on phrases that might make us feel like we're wrong for feeling how we feel (you cannot be wrong for how you feel, by the way), I suggest we instead give influence to mottos that draw our attention to things we can *actually* control.

How about this one:

Become the person that the person you're
looking for is looking for.
– Andy Stanley

When I met Aaron, it wasn't on schedule, it wasn't when I was out on the prowl, and it wasn't during a time I could realistically start building anything with him (hence the month-long hiatus while I figured out my life). But I'd set myself up for success because I'd finally taken the reins of my life. Both literally and figuratively—remember the horseback riding lessons? That deliberate step toward happiness turned out to be an attractive quality. Who woulda thunk. Making the decision to move to a new city? Also attractive, because we are drawn to people who actively live life instead of passively let life "happen" to them.

When chatting that first night, Aaron learned that I had bachelorette parties to attend and goodbye brunches to plan in the coming weeks. My life was full of change, hobbies, and friend-events. I'd recently emerged from a heartbreak that took me nine months to mend, so ironically, I was pretty passive about my love life for the first time…maybe ever? Didn't want to deal with *that* again. Therefore, I didn't feel the need to keep in touch with the hot guy from Virginia Beach, because my life already had momentum and a happily repaired, fully functioning heart.

I've never, not once, been attracted to someone who isn't living a life with momentum and wholeness. I don't want to be somebody's All! That is too much pressure. No, I want someone who has friends and plans and a life. I think this is what the whole "love yourself first" mantra is getting at, but if you sit around trying to pressure yourself to love yourself, you'll forget to get out there and just do things you love! Creating a life you love *is* how you love yourself!

Think about the kind of person *you* want to spend your life with. Is he friendly? Secure in his political or religious beliefs? Funny? Kind? Diligent? Talented? Let those descriptors lead you toward your *own* actions, and you might be surprised to find yourself surrounded by the right fish in the sea.

THERE'S NO SUCH THING AS PERFECT

There's a difference between someone being right for you and someone being perfect.

Am I the only one who rolls my eyes when someone says they're single because they're "too picky"? Or that they have "really high standards"?

Listen, I don't condone diving into a marriage just for the sake of booking a trendy engagement photo session. Nor can I ignore the dangers of being swept away by lust and emotion or the fulfillment of an insecurity. Standards are necessary. Caution is wise. Self-awareness is crucial.

But tread lightly on the concept of expecting your significant other to be paper perfect. Love is not an excel sheet. You cannot treat a human being as a checklist.

In the age of endless options and a checkbox mentality, we think we can simply find someone "better" if our significant other isn't measuring up. In fact, we can divorce someone the second they're not "making us happy," and society tells us that's a perfectly reasonable—nay, respectable—thing to do.

Whewee folks, I smell danger. It is dangerous to expect our

relationships to measure up to a particular ideal, especially if that ideal is based on feel-good quotes, modern philosophies about happiness (has anyone noticed the world is actually more depressed than ever?), or comparison. It's misguided to believe that love doesn't ebb and flow, or that your feelings are not direct results of your actions (or inaction). If both parties are willing—and I do recognize the magnitude of that "if"—it's entirely possible to wade the murky waters of failed expectations and grow into an even more rooted, connected couple.

Of course I want you to be in a relationship that meets your needs, with someone who is respectful, kind, and the exact doppelganger of Chris Hemsworth. And deal breakers aren't bad. I am not talking about putting up with abuse, manipulation, or betrayal. I'm not even talking about red flags before you go all in with commitment.

I'm saying this: You cannot expect your partner to be your Everything, because he is not God. You cannot expect him to be perfect, because he is not a Chipotle burrito bowl with extra guac. You cannot expect to not get hurt on some level, to always agree, to never get bored, to always be in the mood for sex, to communicate clearly, to understand intentions, or for that person to magically warp into your friend's husband who always gives her backrubs on Sunday mornings.

You must be realistic in accepting that you will be dating or married to a real life human being with a unique fingerprint. He will never be the sugarcoated dreamboat clone you read about in mushy Facebook statuses.

Get this: The top 5 words or phrases women use to describe their husbands on Twitter are "the best," "my best friend," "amazing," "the greatest," and "so cute." The top 5 words women use when Googling information about their husband are "gay," "a jerk," "amazing," "annoying," and "mean."

What people share publicly about their relationships—particularly on social media—does not fairly represent what's actually going on behind the scenes. If you find yourself falling into the trap of wishing your relationship was like so-and-so's, just remind yourself that she probably thinks her husband is gay. Problem solved!

I also think that society is ruining us by preaching presumptuous decrees about what makes women "strong" in terms of a relationship: *No self-respecting, strong woman is going to put up with a man who doesn't follow up on his text message or can't articulate his well-informed thoughts on every social issue or doesn't put his clothes in the laundry bin!*

Red flags are red flags, yes. Respect is vital, duh. And before you get married, I highly recommend conversations about who's in charge of the laundry and what you believe about church and state. BUT. Sometimes a really fantastic guy will simply drop the ball. It doesn't mean he's a disrespectful, immature, or unreliable person—it might just mean he has some aloof tendencies, is occasionally indecisive, or potentially needs a simple, clear lesson.

Here's a prime example: For our second date, my husband and I were meeting at a private party where he'd been granted a plus one. Instead of him picking me up, we agreed to separately Uber to the location, as we'd both be taking advantage of the open bar. (Heyoo!) Since I wasn't allowed inside without him and only lived a four-minute drive away, he told me he'd text me when he arrived, at which point I could call my Uber to come join him.

He was supposed to text around 6:00 p.m.

I waited.

It was 6:10 p.m. Then 6:25. Then 6:40.

I waited a full hour.

I could've assumed the silence meant he didn't care if I showed—or worse, that he didn't want me there. But instead, I finally texted him to make sure he hadn't been murdered by his Uber driver, swallowed my frustration when he casually responded, "Yeah, I'm here! Come whenever!" and showed up anyway.

Now, you better believe we've had plenty of conversations since then about his distracted tendencies (Him: *But* honey *there was an ice luge at that party!*), but I'm glad I didn't write him off because he goofed in the beginning. He may have forgotten to tell me to show up for our date because he was too busy sucking vodka from a frozen sculpture, but that night ended up solidifying our feelings for each other and is one of the main reasons the rest of our relationship unfolded as it did.

It's very true that in some cases, if a person behaves with disrespect or perceived disinterest, he isn't in it to win it. But it's worth putting aside "pickiness" to give someone a second chance, recognizing that sometimes a character flaw—like my husband's easily distracted nature—is not always a trait that outweighs his valuable qualities. Plenty of people deserve to be dropped if they continually show signs of disregard or incompatibility, but offering grace isn't a sign of weakness. There is a difference between red flags and flawed humanity.

MANAGING EXPECTATIONS

Once inside committed relationships, expectations can be whittled down into three categories: Sex, communication, and responsibilities. Let's unpack them a bit, shall we?

1. SEX

Bumping dirties is not something I choose to talk about publicly. With my friends? Oh man. I am disgusting and offer far too much detail about both the emotional and physical intricacies of all things Bedroom. But for a public forum—let's say, oh, a book that my dad will have access to? Not my thing.

I would do the classic "Dad, please skip this chapter" plea, but I know my father, and he will want to read every last word of this book, so Dad, just don't bring any of this up in person, capiche? Also, this is me retaliating because of that one time you got tipsy and told me where I was conceived. Gross.

Actually—I hate to disappoint—but not much of what I want to say here is about my own experience between the sheets. You dirty dogs. I'd really just like to crack the code as to why so many of us feel insecure about our sex lives, particularly in our marriages. The most obvious reason is that, as with literally every subject discussed in this book, we are holding ourselves to a gold standard that is both arbitrary and misrepresented.

You've likely heard one or all of the following, even if just inside your own head:

You're not having enough sex, therefore lessening your bond.

You're having too much sex and using it as a crutch for an otherwise dysfunctional relationship.

If you don't show interest as often as your partner, you're partially to blame if they fill their needs elsewhere.

Your sex life lacks passion. Be more creative.

You need to keep it interesting. Keep it often. Keep it healthy and easy and confident and engaged and and and...

Whoa. Sex was never intended to withstand all of these expectations. It is a private experience between two adults. How it infiltrates each relationship can and should be entirely different. So what if your friend has sex with her husband four times a week? So what if your favorite life coach says your relationship is doomed if you don't figure out how to climax every time? How about this—how about we look at sex as it pertains to *you*? To your history and relationship and circumstances. Screw the rest. Pun intended.

I don't think anyone would say that sex *doesn't* matter in marriage. It does! In fact, isn't sexual attraction the primary differentiation between a relationship and a friendship? Sexual arousal definitely sets my relationship with my husband apart from my girlfriends. (Sorry, ladies.) But the way you handle that aspect of your relationship is entirely between you and your partner. Comparing yourself to that couple that swears they never lost the "spark" after 20 years is not only pointless, but it's also probably based on a lie.

According to data analysts, there are sixteen times the complaints on search engines reflecting a spouse not wanting to engage in sex than there are searches about a spouse not wanting to communicate. That's a heck of a lot more people wondering why their spouse won't have sex with them over why they won't talk to them! Clearly this is important to people—and a common issue.

Here's the even bigger *Come again??* moment (pun not intended, ew): *Twice* as many searches complain that a boyfriend won't have sex than that a girlfriend won't have sex. Now, that might not mean that's twice as likely a scenario—maybe women are more prone to Googling solutions to their problems, and we should account for same-sex relationships—but this information still indicates that a man not wanting constant sex in a relationship is more frequent than we tend to believe. So if your insecurities tell you that all men are wired to go at it 24/7, realize it's not about you, and you're certainly not alone.

Yes, sex is very much about two people, but it's just as much about each party's autonomous, ever-changing state of being. If you're the one struggling with drive, identifying a cause outside of your current relationship often helps with the guilt and pressure. We can't ignore the fact that our histories of emotions associated with sex can come into play.

Perhaps you had many sexual partners before marriage and now have to adjust your mindset about monogamy and meaning. Then there's depression, stress, abuse, physical pain, insecurities, and an endless array of potential roadblocks. Why would we assume that everyone can manage those challenges in a manner that always leads back to an easy, happy little sex life? Clearly, sex isn't always a reflection of how in love you are. Thus, if we let our love become defined by sex—if we mistakenly use it as a metric—we potentially let the love itself die on a [unused] bed of roses instead of helping it grow through patience and exploration.

Maintaining closeness through sex is just like any other rewarding and fulfilling experience in life—it requires commitment, consistency, and the right perspective. Newness is always sexy. Once that's gone, friend, you've got to be willing to find another means to the end.

Chalking *anything* up to "it should come easily" is a disillusioned and ultimately disheartening way to walk through life. That's simply not the way life works. You'll end up wondering why you're so darn unlucky and unhappy all the time. (I will make the exception that getting along with your spouse on a basic level should come pretty easily—especially at the beginning—as a foundation for a healthy relationship. This whole Hollywood romanticism of emotional turmoil equating passion is plain exhausting and usually disastrous.)

The purpose of sex, at least according to my own doctrine and experience, is to provide pleasure in a way that leaves you feeling closer to the other person. Not resentful. Not proud. Not wanted or taken care of or even satisfied. Those last results are byproducts of healthy sex, but they are not the purpose. Sex doesn't always have to be some drawn out love-making ordeal, but its design is always about unity.

I've absolutely found myself in stages of my relationship where I view sex as a necessary way to make my husband happy. A thing that I simply don't feel like doing, but know I should. I start to see it as this ingredient of being a good wife, and a way to reflect the fact that I love my husband. I forget to be grateful for it. To remove the pressure I feel and think of it as a gift that will allow me to connect with him, not just "be good to him." Sex is an opportunity, not an obligation.

Last note on this never-not-awkward expectation—because repetition is important—for the love of all things holy (which includes sex), go ahead and bang your head against a wall until you accept that your sex life is not comparable to anyone else's. Don't take that literally, please, because I care about you, but figuratively *beat that out of your head.* Taking advice is fine, but you do not need to follow the same path that worked for someone else, or God forbid come to unnecessary conclusions about your marriage based on a couple whose marital issues don't live in the bedroom. Focus on yourself, your partner, and embracing the unity God intended.

You *can* figure this out. Be open to change, consistent in your personal growth, and patient with your partner. Read some books, go to therapy, and get on a freakin' treadmill. Oh, and sleep naked. Just try it.

2. COMMUNICATION

I love confrontation. Not unhealthy, combative confrontation, but let's-address-the-issue-so-it-can-change confrontation. For better or worse, God gave me zero fear in the interpersonal department, and I'm here for it.

Without my love for all things communication, I probably wouldn't write this book or make friends with the pizza delivery people on the phone or know how my husband *actually* feels about Alfredo sauce.

Now, communication doesn't mean talking for the sake of talking or over-analyzing to the point of misconceptions. In fact, I can't handle long bouts of pointless communication. Sitting next to a stranger at a wedding makes me want to hide. I'm outgoing and love to talk through interpersonal issues, however I completely lose energy from small talk. My husband, on the other hand, gains energy from casual human interaction, yet it's like scraping burnt chicken off a stainless steel pan to get the man to verbalize his true feelings. This is a fun dynamic.

Whether we realize it or not, we're always communicating—it's just a matter of whether or not we're doing it *well.* Even if you haven't had a real conversation with your spouse in years, that silence communicates plenty. Thus, it's important to begin this section on communication by recognizing that communication isn't something you can get out of. It's not a choice or a goal—it's simply a reality that comes with being alive and around other human beings.

When we're not communicating intentionally, odds are our lives are full of misunderstandings, internal or overt frustration, and loneliness. If we are not being seen or interpreted for the way we truly feel and think, not only are our relationships built upon assumptions, but no one knows our souls. It's isolating.

If we refuse to humbly learn the inner workings of other people simply because it's uncomfortable, inconvenient, or too much work, then we're lying to ourselves about what it means to love someone. Either you indulge in your own comfort, or you indulge in the needs and hearts of people you love. You don't even have to change your mind on a matter or fully understand why their heart and mind work how they do, but you *do* have to be willing to listen and let their truth affect your actions in how you exhibit love.

Loving someone unconditionally is not just that you'll always invite them to dinner, be more or less kind to them, and remain loyal. No. Loving someone unconditionally is to be truly familiar with them, to acknowledge their truth even if it's hard for you to relate, and respond to their vulnerability in a way that reflects respect, care, and humility. *That* is unconditional love. And how is it achieved? Communication.

Communication is the root of human connection, and what human should you be more connected to (besides yourself) than your significant other?

In a shocking twist as totally unpredictable as the big city woman ending up with the small town guy in a Hallmark movie, communication is going to look and work different for each couple. This is your life. Your love. Your story.

Lead with your own vulnerability, and let the conversation unfold without accusations or vocalizing some general mission to "communicate better." The way we refer to communication in relationships has become so vague and broad that it's more of a buzzword than an actual cornerstone.

To be more specific about what communication behaviors have proven most telling of a lasting relationship (hint: it's not writing the longest caption on Valentine's Day), we can look at the work of John Gottman, a researcher and marriage expert who separates couples into two distinct categories: Masters and Disasters.

In case those names aren't obvious, couples in the Masters category have a close friendship that is supplemented with romantic intimacy, connection, and an intentional and true awareness of what's going on in the life of the other person. Disasters are the dysfunctional couples who feel emotionally and potentially physically isolated from their spouse, and don't have a sense of authenticity or self within that relationship.

The measuring factors between these two types of couples boil down to two statistics:

Masters—i.e. healthy couples projected to last—show a 5:1 ratio of compliments compared to negative comments. For every snide remark, complaint, or criticism, there are five or more loving interactions to counteract the bad stuff. These positive comments can be as simple as thank yous, apologies, offers to help, compliments, phrases of adoration (my brother's personal favorite for his wife: "Baby you're so hot"…it's basically a family drinking game at this point), or genuine requests for forgiveness—any verbal communication that moves the relationship forward in a positive manner.

Masters also respond to their spouse 9 out of 10 times. Meaning, if a spouse makes a request for attention, then nearly every single time, the other person acknowledges them. Requests for attention look like sharing a funny meme, pointing out a deer in the backyard, commenting on the news, discussing a child's behavior, telling a story about the office drama queen—anything that would illicit a response or engagement. None of us respond every single time because maybe our face is in our phone or our mind is distracted or we don't hear them, but if it's a very typical pattern to engage in a response to something your spouse says, therefore showing interest in what's important enough for them to say out loud, then you are likely in a Masters situation. Ten points Gryffindor!

To plainly paint the whole picture, Disasters interact with fewer positive comments to combat the negative, and more frequently ignore each other's observations.

So at least nod and agree that Chad sounds like an annoying coworker.

Communication is more than honest conversations about major issues—it's about daily, habitual responses and reactions to create an ease of living around your partner. Be cute, be kind, be cognizant. Someone put that on a refrigerator magnet. (Or a dish towel? I digress.)

3. RESPONSIBILITIES

We have expectations surrounding sex. We have expectations surrounding communication. And boy, do we have expectations surrounding basic adulting (v.). From coming up with what to eat for dinner (why is this one of the most overwhelming parts of adulthood??) to remembering trash day, it's the little things that build up or tear down so many relationships.

For the first three and a half years of marriage, Aaron was gone half the year. His ship would leave for two months and return for two months on an endless cycle. While he was off busting drug runners on the open sea with limited email communication, I was home with our infant, slowly figuring out how to consistently shower, feed myself, nurse the baby, develop a sleep schedule, stay on top of laundry, bring Anders to and from the office with me each day, change out the porch light bulb, fix the water filter on the fridge, and make doctors appointments, dog grooming appointments, yard guy appointments, and every other possible appointment on this planet.

With the exception of automatic bills Aaron set up each month, I was keeping our life afloat all on my own. As people like to point out, "it's what you sign up for" when you become a military spouse. Which is perhaps the most misguided and annoying phrase you can say to someone, so let's not.

What people don't see is what happens when a military spouse returns home, and how that affects the fragile balancing act of responsibilities that is so heavily one-sided while they're away.

The first week of his return after each two-month patrol, everyone would say, "Oh it must be so amazing to have Aaron home again!!" Yes, I was always thrilled to have him back. I love him, and he's my favorite person to be around.

BUT.

The first week he got home was always the absolute worst.

A major part of me felt more exhausted by managing a third body in the house than relieved to be reunited with my husband. *Stop adding more laundry to the pile, more dishes to the sink, more interaction I need to engage in instead of quietly folding the laundry while watching* This is Us, *and for the LOVE OF PETE stop asking me questions about all the things I'm doing as if I need to explain why or how I kept this family and house upright the last 60 days.*

I'm such a sweet wife. Welcome home, honey.

The other part of me would suddenly feel completely unmotivated to do anything at all. I wanted to drop this entire heavy weight of responsibilities now that my partner was home. You know—let him make up for lost time. I would hardly ever let the laundry or dishes build up when he was gone, but now? Welp, he can do it if he wants a clean spoon for his cereal. He can call the yard guys or mow the dang grass himself. He can come up with dinner ideas and replace the wipes in the diaper drawer and figure out why the light on our fridge keeps flashing.

Resentment is a sneaky little booger, isn't it?

I'd vacillate between a self-righteous I-can-do-it-all attitude and being a complete bump on a log. Meanwhile, Aaron was just trying to keep his head afloat with relearning ever-changing information about his baby, remembering all the things that needed to be done every day, and staying on top of my wavering expectations.

The tension was brutal. No matter how many times we tried to prepare ourselves for these transition weeks, never once did we get through one without biting each other's heads off.

I take full responsibility for the poor hand-off of shared responsibilities. My expectations were never firmly in place, therefore he was always stuck trying to figure out what would make me happy. He's generous like that. The problem was that *I* didn't even know what would make me happy. I wanted all the control and also none of it. Eventually we'd settle back into a routine, but the expectation of who would do what was a *mess* each time we had to reestablish our lives together. Every eight weeks.

Not a big fan of that work schedule.

Basic responsibilities can wreak havoc on a relationship if not clearly defined and executed. This isn't to say we shouldn't keep an eye out for opportunities to help one another on the fly, but generally speaking: Make a doggone plan.

Naming specific needs and addressing who should manage what is way easier than mind reading. I know he should replace the stupid toilet paper roll without being asked, but do you really want your stubbornness in "I shouldn't have to say something" be the demise of your relationship? Just *say something*! Calmly.

This leads me to one of my favorite topics: Income isn't

hierarchy. Let me break it down for my slackers in the back! *You cannot allocate responsibilities based on who is making all or more of the money*. Changing a toilet paper roll is not beneath anyone.

Identifying one person's responsibility as "the house" and the other's as "the money" completely nullifies the reality of a dynamic family unit. To justify disinterest in the daily lives of your family or upkeep of your home simply because you make the money is not only selfish and unloving, but you are wasting the most fulfilling and significant part of your life, which is to engage with the people you love. Yes, that means by clearing the dinner table.

Before I get too wrapped up in the antiquated and audacious pattern of the moneymaker somehow claiming more rights to basic human needs like sleep, personal time, and affection, let me regroup.

Responsibilities have to be specific and habitual. Dual income homes require even more communication, since it'd be far too easy to fall into the "let's just split responsibilities evenly" fake-plan. It's like a group project—one person will inevitably do more, whether it's because they're a control freak or because they think, "If I don't do it, so-and-so will."

Assigning specific roles might sound elementary, but trust me—it works. Again, this doesn't mean you never cross roles or help the other person out, but a general routine of divided responsibilities brings a tremendous amount of peace to a household.

Responsibilities aren't just household chores, by the way. We might think our husband is responsible for cutting back on the social drinking now that he's married. We might think our spouse is responsible for remembering our mom's birthday or sucking it up for a chick flick. Life is full of random behavioral expectations that we consciously or subconsciously expect our spouse to keep up with. It's all too easy to assume that a piece of paper legally binding us together will magically transform someone into behaving more "husbandly" or "wifely." *Surely he won't keep playing beer pong every Friday night with his buddies once he has a ring on it! Surely she will learn to cook once we have children!*

I've got some news: There is no magic switch that makes someone more responsible once they enter a legal union. We bring our individual selves into a marriage, and as much as we should be aware of how our behavior now affects another individual, that doesn't mean our habits, flaws, and skills are suddenly warped into perfection. We also bring our own ideas of what a marriage looks like into the relationship, which is usually not perfectly aligned with the other person's vision. In the name of love, commitment, and growth, we have to be willing to make personal changes and relational compromises.

This feels like the perfect opportunity to introduce one of my marriage's most sticky subjects: Time.

I love to be on time. And I'm not just talking about picking up my kid at daycare before they charge me extra, or showing up to a friend's house for dinner when we planned. I mean that I love to make arbitrary time goals for every single event. I want to finish dinner by 6 p.m. I want to leave the house to make my Starbucks run by 7:15 a.m. I want to be home from the grocery store by 11:30 a.m. so that I can write 1500 words by 1 p.m. I am so attached to a clock, it's scary—especially for my husband, who, despite his military experience, views clocks as vague institutions of science invented to remind us that the world has an axis.

I'll never forget spending my first Thanksgiving with his family, and his sister was hosting. She said dinner would be served at 5 p.m. Around 2 p.m., Aaron and his parents drove me to their favorite Ohio landmark, Lehman's (Aaron calls it the "Amish Walmart"), which was 1.5 hours away from my sister-in-law's house. I kept looking at the clock. *How will this work? That's three hours of driving! And we only have three hours before dinner. So does this mean we aren't really going to shop? Or is someone just running in to grab something?*

Once it was 4 p.m. and we were still moseying around the store, I was in full panic mode.

I finally pulled Aaron aside and said, "Does anyone realize what time it is?? Your sister is going to kill us! We'll never make it to her house in time for dinner!" Aaron—cool as a cucumber—laughed and said, "Don't worry, 5 p.m. just means 'in the evening at some point.'"

I'm sorry, what??

In my family's home, 5 p.m. means 5 p.m. butts-in-seats, wine already poured, be there or be square. I was utterly shocked and unaware that some folks go through life with their cortisol levels entirely unaffected by the numbers on a clock.

Now imagine how that completely different view of time has affected the joining of our lives in marriage. Let me tell you, during the first few years, getting my husband out of the house was among the most maddening experiences of my life. When I went into quickly-escalating labor with our first child and the car had been packed for weeks, it *still* was like herding cattle, except Aaron was the only cow. Somehow more scattered than an entire herd. All we needed to grab were some toiletries and scoot on out the door so that this baby could arrive *not* in our living room.

You guys. I waited over *30 minutes* once my water broke with ever-increasing contractions before I finally hollered up the stairs and insisted he come *get in the dang car*. To this day, I do not know what he was doing up there while I prepared for my body to expel a live human, but my strained voice was finally enough to get him out the door.

Aaron's relationship with a clock has changed drastically in the last five years. He's still prone to dilly-dallying and "time expanding," as I call it—when you somehow fill every second of time you have, even if your task normally takes less time to complete—but he has seen how much this behavior stresses me out. Out of love and respect, he has made some pretty remarkable headway. On the flip side, I've become less militaristic, racing the clock less often and taking deep breaths when necessary.

You didn't marry your clone, so stop holding the bar for your spouse at a standard only you, yourself could naturally meet. (Let's be real, you'd fall short, too.)

And keep in mind your spouse isn't a character in a movie or the highlight reel of someone else's life, either. If you expect the empty milk carton to not find its way back into the fridge, you might just need to ask.

NO GUARANTEES

...National surveys indicate that 15 percent of married women and 25 percent of married men have had extramarital affairs. The incidence is about 20 percent higher when emotional and sexual relationships without intercourse are included.

– Jane E. Brody,
"When a Partner Cheats," *The New York Times,* 2018

While we're on the subject of feeling behind in life due to our relationship (or lack there of), we might as well face the sobering fact that just because someone's in a relationship right now doesn't mean they're "ahead."

Hearing that 1 in 4 married men have physically cheated on their wives—and almost 1 in 6 married women have done the same—is pretty jarring. You probably know more than four married men or more than six married women. Do the math. Whether or not they air it in uncomfortable vaguebook statuses, odds are not every marriage is as dandy as you think. But you probably know this. After all, the fear of a bad marriage is why so many millennials wait so long to get married in the first place!

And still, how many of us subconsciously assume that all married people are as happy as they look in pictures? Or that despite the troubles you've witnessed first-hand, *at least they have each other.*

Us weirdo humans have this uncanny ability to bestow the assumption of good fortune onto other people, while we don the crown of short sticks. I'm not sure why we do this—as though we're determined to believe our lives don't measure up. Perhaps it gives us something to look forward to, or maybe it's just the devil trying to steal our joy. Whatever the reason, it's unproductive.

Now don't go judging other people's marriages just because I told you that they're not always what they're cracked up to be. In fact, since we know that many marriages will end up in divorce (39% according to latest trends—better than in the '80s!), we should be all the *more* inclined to support one another. Whether single, in a relationship, or married, we have *got* to look out for one another. We cannot assume everyone around us is okay, that their hearts aren't being broken, or that they're safe, happy, free, and whole. (And if they are, that deserves genuine celebration! Cheers!)

MINI-MOON IS NOT A WORD

I have to talk about weddings real fast. I cannot help myself. Relationships go through a million stages that lend themselves to comparison, but the single most concentrated moment highlighting each relationship is the wedding day. After all, it's when everyone comes together to celebrate this commitment to love, so naturally we see it as the most important event in a couple's life!

News flash—it's not. Not even close.

Despite their fleeting nature, weddings constantly make couples feel inferior, prepping them for an endless cycle of feeling behind throughout their entire marriage.

Let's start with the obvious. If you feel like your marriage is off to a rocky start because you can't afford three protein options for your guests, flowers on every table, a custom gown, a wedding video worthy of Netflix, a cake with at least four tiers, a limo to drive you around, and Pinterest-worthy décor—I'm here to let you off the hook. Please, please step away from social media. We all know it's a bunch of hocus pocus, yet we're addicted to creating the "magic."

What's the popular phrase? Oh: *Your wedding should feel like "you"...?* What does that even mean?! Who am I? I guess it means I need enough DIY elements to prove I'm creative and dedicated, the ambiance of my favorite Disney Princess' ball scene, and koozie party favors because we're such a fun couple. *Can't you see how fun we are??*

I actually love our wedding koozie but that's neither here nor there. #partyleykorockstar

This hoopla is for what—to prove we're worthy of love? To prove to everyone invited that we're cool? Shouldn't they already think you're cool if they're coming to your wedding? It doesn't even make sense, you guys!

Stop it. Stop giving consumerism and comparison what it wants! Don't give in!! Your wedding is about your marriage! You know it, I know it, and we all roll our eyes about over-the-top weddings—yet the vast majority of us still try to keep up with the Joneses amidst the eye rolling. It's absolutely ridiculous!

Listen, I love planning, I love pretty things, I love crafting, and I love getting my loved ones in the same room. I was lucky to have a large wedding, and I have no regrets. I'm not insulting big, beautiful weddings. It was my favorite day. But if you someday run across someone who attended mine, I challenge you to ask them if they had flowers on their table or if they remember what the cake looked like. They probably even lost their stinking koozie.

I'll let you in on a secret: We didn't have flowers on every table, and our display cake was pretty small—most of the edible pieces came from a secret sheet cake in the back kitchen. Everyone got chicken. *Everyone*. Also, there was no flower girl or ring bearer or pew decorations. The string quartet played the wrong song as I walked down the aisle. I bought the first dress I tried on off a clearance rack at a bridal shop going out of business. I didn't do a single hair or makeup trial. My gift to my bridesmaids were earrings Aaron made himself, and instead of using a limo, we called an Uber to pick us up after our exit from the reception.

Who freaking cares?? I mean, seriously. This is about gathering loved ones to witness the promise you're making to the person you love, committing the rest of your days here on earth to be spent with that *one* person.

If you like the traditions that come with the wedding day (like me)—great! Do what you can to honor them, but don't freak out if your bouquet is small. Let some things go, girlfriend. No one cares but you. If they do, they shouldn't be on the guest list anyway.

If you're a courthouse or backyard kind of gal, own it. If you wish you had a fairytale budget but don't, please realize it's not worth the debt! Hang some string lights in a fellowship hall and call it a night! Focus on the love between you and your fiancé, and the rest will blur into the background over the years, I promise you that.

And never—I mean *never*—use the term "mini-moon." I have all the feelings on this recently invented label that is the ultimate wedding-related societal coercion to be the most lofty, envy-worthy couple on Instagram. I have friends who I love dearly who use this term, so I don't hate the player—I just *hate* the game.

If you're calling your five-day getaway to another city (or even another country) a mini-moon because God forbid your real honeymoon not be a two-week vacation in a location only accessible by NASA or floo powder, then you need to evaluate a few things.

One, you need to evaluate the purpose of a honeymoon. Is it to spend some alone time with your new spouse, really leaning into the vows you just made to each other? Or is it to take pictures and prove to your followers and friends that you're living your #bestlife?

Two, you need to evaluate your privilege, and the way that privilege makes other people feel. If you want to spend a long weekend at a Bed & Breakfast after your wedding, then fly to Thailand six months later, that's fine. But the Bed & Breakfast is your honeymoon. Thailand is a vacation you take with your spouse. By downplaying the Bed & Breakfast as a mini-moon, you're completely degrading couples whose "only" honeymoon consists of the same thing. Heck, I know people who call their mini-moon a full week in the Bahamas, or a full week in Miami.

I thought I was pretty darn blessed to take a weeklong honeymoon in Mexico with Aaron. But now I'm inadvertently told that's only mini-moon status? Am I going crazy here, or does anyone else agree that our society has gone absolutely bonkers with the pressure to all act like we're one-percenters?

The wedding, the honeymoon, the entire relationship is about love! Two people choosing to walk through the challenges and successes of life together, in this *one* life we have to live. ONE! Our single string of days that will someday come to an end, and we're saying that we want to share those precious days with another person until our dying breath.

Please tell me what that has to do with cake or seating chart displays or Lake Como?

Whew, lovebirds, can we get it together? Let's remove the pressure from day one of marriage so that the rest of our lives aren't built upon the sand.

CHAPTER 2

career

WE CAN'T ALL BE OPRAH

When did careers become a thing? Back in the good ole days, I assume that one became a farmer because his father was a farmer and his father's father was a farmer. Or one became a writer because he had nothing more pressing to do with his inheritance of both time and money, or perhaps because he was bored when out tending to the sheep. (Were shepherds literate? I don't know.)

Notice I say "he," because women weren't really in the whole "career world" until less than a century ago. Once we entered the arena, it had already shifted from inherited trade to a bustling business of "discovering your path." Our options of "discovery" were basically limited to teacher, secretary, or nurse, but between those three vocations, it was pick your own adventure!

As a whole, we now approach livelihood from a place of choice rather than in-born responsibility.

Poor Prince Harry.

It's kind of a weird idea, if you think about it, to spend 18 years being told you can "be" anything you want to "be"—language that so recklessly combines self with salary—then all at once, you're expected to know exactly what that is.

Maybe you get one year of wiggle room during your freshman year of college to explore the depths of a keg before declaring a major, but generally speaking, you're supposed to know the basic trajectory of your life just a few months after you had to raise your hand to use the bathroom during senior year homeroom. College or not.

My generation offers a little more lenience toward the whole "finding yourself" phase, whatever that means. As older millennials—not to be confused with younger millennials and Gen Z-ers who had social media in high school and are therefore a completely different breed—my peers and yes, the kidlings after us, don't flinch at flying to Europe when we've yet to establish a 401k. And we not-so-secretly view our first job as a way to pass the time before kickstarting our *actual* career—elusive as that may be. Boomer employers just *love* us!

Even still, we can't escape the nagging feeling that everyone else has a path, or at least a foothold that will lead them to success and establishment. Meanwhile, we're serving (read: eating) baskets of fried pickles in the kitchen at Cheeseburger in Paradise, hoping no one notices that our five-year plan is as loose as the change those A-holes left for a tip.

Ah, I remember those days so vividly. That B.A. in psychology looked *real* cute in the bottom drawer of my childhood desk.

If there's one thing I learned from my 10 year high school reunion, it's that no one has any idea what their career is supposed to look like in their 20s. Not a one. Sure, some of my peers had already spent years in medical school, and others had their real estate licenses or snowboard instructing certifications, but we were all a bit lost as we sipped beers in the local brewery that didn't exist back when we had lockers.

I learned that my peers who were making 70k in an office while I was stealing sweet potato fries from my employer were now considering opening a Soul Cycle franchise. The ones who went to law school still couldn't tell me exactly what corporate law means, or if Sarah over there should hire them for her divorce. I, at the time of the reunion, was proudly touting the role of executive assistant to a wealthy man who owned five different small businesses, and let me tell you—it was hard to explain what that job actually entailed. In fact, I still don't know.

This makes sense given that the average number of jobs in a lifetime is 12, according to a 2019 report. Twelve! You're allowed to figure it out as you go, folks. Everyone else is, too.

We've been bred into a culture that defines us by what we "do," despite the fact that most of us either don't know what we're doing, hate what we're doing, or wonder if what we're doing actually matters.

Maybe you've landed on a career path you love (props!), but doesn't it irk you when people assume that's *all* you are? Like your career is a title that outranks anything unique about your personality or preferences? Bleh—what a bland way to get to know the people around us.

Taking pride in your work is awesome. Enjoying your work

is awesome. But to be defined only by what puts a roof over your head is to ignore the soul beneath it all.

Most of us will never find that "thing" we're good at, that also pays for annual trips to Hawaii and simultaneously saves starving children in Africa. This trifecta of tapped-into-talent, high income, and grandiose mission is the exception, not the rule. Good for Oprah, but let's not get ahead of ourselves here.

This isn't to say you shouldn't pursue avenues at which your passion and talent meet, nor is it impossible to truly change the world or make a billion dollars. In fact, I encourage everyone to find a job that doesn't make them want to hide away and cry every Monday morning. Aiming high is commendable, but why oh why can't we lay off the self-criticism if we end up in a career that isn't flashy or particularly lucrative? Why can't we set aside the self-loathing if we start over with a new profession in our 30s? That doesn't mean everything you've done is a waste. No! The point of a job is to exchange work for money in order to afford food, clothing, a roof, and perhaps essential oils that girl on Instagram convinced you to buy.

The point of *life*—not a job—is to grow. To be kind. To laugh hard with friends, learn about wine regions and what qualifies as an "earthy note," sew a beanie, and cook dinner for the single, tired mom who lives next door. To engage with our world, our creative talents, our minds, and our souls. If some of those things overlap with your career—awesome! But you can succeed at achieving the point of life if you're a hairdresser or a lumberjack or a high school Calculus teacher. Tapping into our ability to love well, serve well, work hard, feed innate creativity, and make change is fundamentally unrelated to what kind of job we hold.

We've got to stop measuring success by LinkedIn profiles and square footage of our homes. Success is found in genuine happiness developed through faith, intentional growth, and human connection. Finding a way to incorporate the cornerstones of life into your career is admirable and certainly ideal, but let's start to separate our worth from our profession. Especially since 99.99% of the people around you who look so put-together aren't Oprah, either.

I CAN'T GET NO (JOB) SATISFACTION

The average American spends 47 hours a week at work. That is about 9 ½ hours a day, five days a week, and doesn't include a commute.

How often do we see our families on workdays? Well, the average American sleeps seven hours a night (yikes—go to bed!), so that leaves us with less than eight hours per day of non-work and non-sleep time. If your kids go to bed early, or you have any form of obligations outside of work—we're looking at spending significantly fewer hours with our loved ones than we do in the office.

Grim.

Given that work is where we spend the largest uninterrupted chunk of our days, no one reading this will be shocked to hear that satisfaction in the workplace spills over into our overall wellbeing and happiness. If we're in an environment full of people we can't stand, doing work that leaves us drained, feeling unappreciated, bored, or stressed to the max, there's no way those feelings don't characterize our lives—especially now that we live in a world where leaving coworkers and work at work is nearly impossible. One second you're putting your kids to bed, and the next second you see your coworker Sheila's thigh rash on Facebook. Can we not?

Fifty-one percent of Americans say they're satisfied in their careers. I'm no mathematical genius, but that tells me that half the people around you are unsatisfied with their work situation. If you are struggling with finding a job that doesn't steal the joy from your life, you are in good company. It doesn't mean there's something wrong with you! Every other person you meet is wondering why they never figured out what they want to be when they grow up, either. I bet if you add stay-at-home moms and currently unemployed folks to the mix, you're looking at a solid majority of the adult population struggling with job satisfaction.

That's pretty bleak. I hate that so many of us are going through life dreading our days. I know it's a privilege to view work as anything other than a paycheck, but I truly do believe each of us has gifts that, if served correctly, could lend themselves to a satisfying career.

Emotional intelligence, patience, creative problem-solving, sharing your faith—all of these (among others) are subtle gifts that easily benefit the workplace. If you find yourself wondering what you love or what you're good at, then perhaps your calling is less obvious than having the voice of Mariah Carey circa 1995. Identify it, harness it, and let it manifest in career success by way of refining your character and improving the lives of those you work with.

But many of you *do* have a more concrete idea of what a dream job looks like. You may have a passion for jewelry, finance, interior design, or doughnuts. Maybe your talents lend themselves to musical theatre, real estate, the military, or filmmaking. If you have a concrete idea or dream in a career sense, I'm here to tell you that it's important. It's not irresponsible, flimsy, embarrassing, or impossible to pursue it. You can agree with me or not, but I believe God gave you these talents and heart-tugs for a reason. To ignore them is to deny the world and your Creator what you have to offer. Do not let your insecurities or your parents or your financial advisor tell you otherwise.

Far too much of our energy is dedicated to following norms and expectations rather than the pull in our bones that guides us toward a life of true fulfillment, tailored to each of our individual talents, personalities, and desires. This goes for career and home life, by the way.

Why are we so afraid? Money? Opinions? Failure? Our fear is driven by weak and subjective terms that can't hold a candle to the spectacular abilities God gifted you.

Let's get specific. Are you afraid you won't make enough money if you pursue a career in line with what you love? Well, who said this dream had to be your primary source of income the very moment you begin pursuing it? Take money out of the equation. Most careers don't turn into careers overnight, so go ahead and do what you need to do to provide for yourself and your dependents, and give your dream the title of Side Hustle.

It won't be flashy, but it *is* possible. Like Henry Ford famously said, "Whether you think you can or you think you can't—you're right." (Side note: I once dated Henry Ford's great great (great?) grandson, even though I did not know his family history when we began dating. Even still, this is fun information that I want to share with the world, so now you know.)

I understand that some of you will have higher mountains to climb based on systemic racism, sexism, and oppression of all kinds, family history, access to education, and location; however, I strongly believe that there is more than one path to success, and it's a matter of identifying your own, even if it's a bit longer or bumpier than someone else's.

By the way—if you have fewer obstacles in your way, why not offer a hand and bring someone else along with you on this journey? Just some food for thought.

Money and resources are one point on the fear triangle, while opinions and failure are the others. You're old enough to read, so you're old enough to know that the opinions of others *should* not hold you back. And yet, it *really* sucks to feel embarrassed when someone on social media calls you annoying or your grandfather implies that you're irresponsible.

Our logic rarely holds its ground against our easily inflated feelings of shame. It's not easy to maintain confidence in the face of criticism when we're already navigating unfamiliar, intimidating territory of our dream job, itself. This is where God comes in. This is where the right relationships come in. This is the moment your personal resolution to live above the noise comes in.

Your dream job may not make you rich or powerful or flashy, and there's no guarantee that just because God puts something on your heart, it will come to fruition. But maybe it's less about the cupcake shop, and more about someone you meet along the way whose life you changed (or changed yours). Maybe it's a lesson learned, a habit formed, or a series of experiences that brought you true happiness.

These alternative victories in no way undermine the magic of committing to your dream until it's reality. I highly recommend consistency and persistence. However, the overarching goal itself is not the measure of success. What pursuing that dream does to your heart and the hearts around you is the true payoff.

IMPOSTER SYNDROME

The lucky half of Americans who are satisfied with their careers are still not immune to the feeling of inadequacy or comparison in the workplace. I'm telling you, this whole concept of being "behind" has infiltrated itself into every nook and cranny, no matter who you are or where you are! Nobody's safe. Hide your kids. Hide your wife.

Almost everyone—particularly women—struggle with imposter syndrome. We privately believe we're underqualified for our position, and are afraid to be "found out." We cling to a façade of perfection to satisfy the ball of nerves rolling around in our stomachs. The self-talk goes like this: *Everyone else has all the answers, so I am a fraud until I do, too.*

Only no one else has all the answers.

We see ourselves as merely human because at night, we undress down to our spiky legs and watch trash television or cyberstalk our exes. How in the world can anyone take us seriously when we know just how lame or weird or indulgent we actually are?

Guys. Gals. We're *all* merely human. That hard core executive who knows all the things? She eats peanut butter out of the jar while watching *The Masked Singer*. The blogger with 700,000 more followers than you? She didn't know how to read a brand contract when she started. Probably still doesn't.

Yes, you need to figure out the hard answers, absorb information, prepare for meetings, research, etc., but your peers and bosses are humans who never use the lettuce in their fridge, either. It's all too easy to think of ourselves as imposters since we're so acutely aware of our humanity, and assume the people around us have these magical minds with insight and fortitude and talent that we don't possess. But that's false! Bill Gates? Human. Beyoncé? Human. Kylie Jenner? Mostly human.

No matter how impressive someone is in their field, they aren't made of magic. (Not counting my girl Hermione Granger.) If you can realize that, then you'll stop expecting yourself to be made of magic, too. No one is going to "find out" that you have never solved a budgeting crisis like this before, or that you're just a mac-and-cheese loving gal who had to Google how to add code in Excel.

You are brilliant. You are capable. And you're allowed to learn.

Education is another offshoot of imposter syndrome. Someone once told me that with a bachelor's degree in psychology, I was officially qualified to be a Starbucks barista. No more, and no less. I think they underestimated how much I love and respect my Starbucks baristas. Alas, I spent at least nine years feeling like my cum laude college graduation was an embarrassment because I still wasn't qualified enough to actually do anything in the field of psychology.

When I got my first office job, I looked around at all the Duke and Dartmouth grads (literally every single person in that office had graduated from one of those two institutions), and assumed they'd majored in "how-to-make-cool-graphics-and-magically-determine-important-consulting-information-for-the-federal-sector." I don't know if that's a major, but it had to be, because I could not comprehend what my peers were doing. I say "peers" lightly. I was the front desk office manager. They were actual associates. I bought them pistachios for the snack bin.

It's not that my bosses didn't give me ample opportunity to transition from greeter to associate. They did, but instead of me recognizing that I have an actual brain, I assumed I was a lost cause because I didn't have the right education. I've always known I'm pretty smart, have never failed at an academic assignment, and am not afraid of hard work. However, I self-sabotaged by not believing in my ability to thrive in this high-energy, high-stakes office environment all because my degree and alma mater didn't seem to hold enough prestige. (Captain for life! Still love ya!)

Now six years removed from that experience, I'm going to assume that the young associates in that office did not have degrees any more conducive to their assignments than mine. They likely had liberal arts degrees with a minor in flip cup, but came into that office with the belief that they could figure it out. That sort of confidence can do wonders in a world where, surprise! We're all winging it.

Knowing you are capable in the workplace isn't about faking perfection or checking a specific education bracket, both which feed imposter syndrome. However, there is some power in fake-it-'til-you-make-it. In feeling confident that you can *figure it out*. We don't want the eggshells type of faking that comes with imposter syndrome. Nah, we want the believing-in-yourself, scrappy kind of wit. That's the antidote to imposter syndrome.

With the exception of landing a waitressing job at a high end Italian steak house in New York City without having ever opened a bottle of wine with a wine key, I didn't learn the art of fake-it-'til-you-make-it until a few years after buying pistachios for those Dartmouth grads.

There I was, floating down a river on an inner tube amidst 50 or so other people, listening to "Livin' on a Prayer" blasting from someone's waterproof speaker. I was 27, six months married, and jobless. I'd recently decided to see if I could monetize my blog, and my husband was kind enough to support me in doing so. I also think he was just tired of hearing me complain about my 9 to 5.

Even though every day was vaca, I was enjoying this river trip, nursing my fourth beer and half-relaxing, half-keeping my eyes peeled for water snakes.

I'd lost track of Aaron and my core group of friends, so my raft was directed by the hand of God and the heart of Te Fiti toward a woman with thick curly hair and a super friendly smile. She was probably 10 or 15 years older than me, and definitely cooler. I introduced myself and learned her name was Swig. Further proof of her coolness.

After verbally untangling the weave of people on the trip to determine who linked us together in this motley crew of tubers, we moved onto other light conversation, like work and babies. (I had neither.) I casually made fun of myself for being a typical millennial who wants to be a blogger. She was very gracious, then casually shared that she was the president of an unscripted television production house. As in, she developed reality TV shows for a living.

SO COOL. I knew it.

Influenced by my Bud Light Limes, I showed no restraint in my enthusiasm. I quickly rambled off all the shows I'm obsessed with—*The Bachelor, The Challenge, Top Chef, Master Chef Junior* (junior is WAY better than the original), *Vanderpump Rules, The Biggest Loser, Fixer Upper*, and the list goes on. I'm sure she was thinking I was vapid and a little bit pitiful, but my energy was that of a golden retriever so she showed at least some level of intrigue. Also, she couldn't really swim away that quickly with a tube attached to her.

"So how do you cast the talent? What networks do you work with? Do you know Chip and Jo?" I chirped.

Through my interrogation, I learned that she used to live in New York City and took a cab with Mindy Kaling to work every morning. This gave me all the thrills! Looking back, this information was definitely a sign that something good was about to happen. I've always said that if I could choose any actress to play me in the movie of my life, it would be Mindy Kaling. Who cares if I'm not Indian-American? It's called *acting*, people. Anyway, I all but asked if she could give me Mindy's phone number.

As our tubes began slowly drifting apart (let's be honest, she was probably heavily paddling away beneath the surface), I told her I'd love to come take a tour of the studio since she happened to be headquartered 20 minutes from my apartment in Virginia Beach. She kindly said "Absolutely!" and that was that.

Much to my surprise in the sober aftermath a week later, I received a message on Facebook from none other than Swig herself, living Queen of Coolness, inviting me to her office to interview for a part-time position. Very part-time. One day a week, to be exact. Who else but an unemployed wannabe blogger could commit to just one day a week? I was stoked. I had no idea what the job was, but sign me up to work in reality TV! *I get to meet Andy Cohen right?*

Turns out the job was eight hours of researching potential talent worthy of their own TV show. Social media, magazines, word of mouth—however I could stumble across interesting people doing interesting things, I could pitch it. If Swig and the director of development liked my pitch, they'd reach out to that person and set up a Skype interview. If the Skype call went well, they'd sign the talent and put together a reel to pitch to the appropriate network (HGTV, Bravo, TLC, you name it).

The two other part-time researchers quietly told me that it's considered a good month if you get one "yes" from the leadership team. Maybe two.

My first month, I got 11.

My best month, I got 19.

I'd say this was shocking, but exactly zero people in my life were surprised that I happened to be extremely gifted at finding talent for reality television. My proclivity for stalking ex-boyfriends had finally manifested itself as something useful while I scoured the internet, following leads from random comments on Instagram or one-off quotes in an article. I got inspiration from airline magazines, hashtags, crazy ideas in my head that I Googled, and even The Weather Channel. My pitch sheets were thorough yet concise, usually with an entire concept for a show laid out alongside the talent I'd scouted.

A few months after I began, Swig offered me a second day of work. She then let me take preliminary phone calls with talent, which capitalized on my ability to make friends with just about anyone. Were my answers to their questions about show direction and compensation really all that accurate? Meh, maybe, maybe not. But I could make vague answers sound really convincing because I really believed in giving people a platform to shine, plus I found the work plain-old fun. That golden retriever energy tended to rub off on whoever I was persuading.

From there, things began to take off, partly due to my talent and hard work, and partly because a position happened to open up. Within a year—despite having a 12-week-old baby at this point—I was offered a full-time role as Assistant Director of Development for the entire unscripted department. And it all began with fan-girling over Mindy Kaling while tipsily floating down a river.

Cool story, but why am I telling you? Because I didn't go to school or have any formal training in television production or development. It wasn't even a world that I thought anything about, other than wondering who writes the date cards on *The Bachelor* because you KNOW that's not Chris Harrison's handwriting. I fully fell into the field of unscripted TV, and ended up having a short-lived, yet successful career that I adored until the time came for me to stay at home with my babies in Alaska. (Though there is plenty of potential talent in this part of the world, let me tell you, so perhaps I really should've stuck with it.)

Education rarely has much to do with whether or not you can thrive at your job. In fact, only 27% of college graduates have a job in a field closely related to their degree. In other words, few people really know what they're doing before they start doing it. Sure, if you're a doctor or a lawyer or doing something that Google and a confident attitude can't cover, you should probably get a formal education (I prefer my medical providers to not fake it until they make it), but as for the rest of us—it's all about paving your own way. On a river. With some Bud Limes by your side.

WHO YOU KNOW

I loathe networking. Small talk is my nemesis. I barely know how to do it, and it almost always devolves into taboo subjects like religion or death because I'm awkward like that.

Still, I've been told I'm a pro at networking. And it's true. I will explain my methods, but first, here's why you should even care about my unconventional knack for networking:

A 2016 LinkedIn survey found that 65-75% of new hires weren't looking for a job when they began their latest role. Of that passive talent pool, 62% of them began new jobs because of an opportunity presented to them as a result of interpersonal networking (as opposed to an internal promotion or being randomly poached on LinkedIn). Even for people actively looking for a new job, the hiring scales still favored those who used their network of friends and colleagues to find work over the traditional blind application process.

That's a lot of information just to say it's pretty darn important to know the right people when it comes to landing the job you want. It's not unfair. It's not unethical. It's just life. Companies are comprised of humans, and humans are wired as relational people. (See Chapter 1.) That's going to bleed over into every aspect of life, career included. Yes, even for you accountants and computer programmers. Put on your people pants!

When most of us hear "networking," we think of dull happy hours arranged by some young professionals group or the age-old advice to "ask someone you admire out for coffee." Technically, is that networking? Sure. But skilled networking is far more natural. It's kind of like the difference between meeting up with a date from Tinder vs. hitting it off with a person you just met at the bar.

Just like talking about relationships on a first date is kind of weird, talking about work with networking prospects is too obvious and forced. Connect on a different level. Talk about your kids. Express your thoughts about the pros and cons of the digital age or reminisce about hand-writing essays in blue books during college. *Can you believe they don't teach kids cursive these days??* The point is: humanize networking.

This is my specialty. I don't do small talk.

Religion. Death. Remember?

Everyone talks about ensuring you "have something to offer," but think about the people you'd help get a job if you were in such a position. It'd be the ones you *like*. Those who seem professional and hardworking, sure, but also the ones you connected with about a sports team or funny bad date story. Better yet, death. Religion.

During the first month I was the office manager at that consulting company full of hungry pistachio smarties, the whole office went on an offsite to a fancy resort called The Greenbrier in West Virginia. The first night, we hosted a cocktail party for clients who were attending a conference at the resort that same weekend (masterful timing). I was so out of my element, it wasn't even funny. If I can barely tell you what my company did *now*, imagine how little I understood *then*. I was in a room full of 100% men who were all discussing federal proposals and mergers and strategy. Twenty-five year old me wanted to dive into a bottle of champagne and die there. Major props to our leadership for including little old me in the offsite, but I was drowning in incomprehensible jargon and uncommon ground.

In a sea of suits emerged a savior. His name was Cameron. He must have sensed my amygdala was beginning to smoke, and graciously guided the conversation toward family instead of business. I ended up telling him that my mother passed a year prior, and in turn he shared that he'd lost his father. (Why can I not *not* talk about death with strangers??) Ignoring the usual protocol for business associations, I mentioned that my mom's faith allowed me to feel more at peace with what happened. Turns out Cameron was a deacon at his church, so we connected on that level, too.

My conversation with just one, relatable human breathed air back into my lungs. I felt seen. No longer inadequate and clueless. Instead, we were just two humans who found common ground. He easily could have brushed me off since I had nothing to offer him in the name of networking, but his kindness changed my entire life.

A few months later, I was desperately trying to find mentorship to reestablish my relationship with God, and thanks to a brief interaction on LinkedIn, Cameron put me in touch with a woman named Annie. To this day, I credit Annie for being God's tool to pull me back into His fold. She helped restore my very wobbly faith that had been tarnished by not only my own choices, but grievances from a previous church (more on that in Chapter 9).

Because of my experience with Cameron and Annie, I became more open about my love for God with other people in my life. Years later, when I became Assistant Director of Development at the production company and I became best friends with my new boss (Swig sadly departed), it was largely due to our shared desire to deepen our faith. The television industry is notoriously difficult to break into, but the door remains open for my future, despite me stepping away for the time being, because my former boss is a mover and shaker in the industry—and still one of my best friends. In fact, she helped me edit this book.

You see, networking isn't just about the person right in front of you. It's about weaving a web of relationships that change your life both professionally and personally. The more you invest in those kinds of interactions, the more advancement you'll experience on and off the corporate ladder.

And if you're convinced you're doomed at the lowest rung of the lowest ladder, might I invite you to feast your eyes on 23-year-old me in a head-to-toe bulky banana costume, flash dancing with 200 other human bananas throughout New

York City to advertise for a smoothie company. Because that happened. Rent ain't cheap!

You're doing just fine. You'll get to the Author stage of your career if you keep your head in the game. You won't be a dancing banana forever.

CHAPTER 3

image

THERE'S MORE TO THE STORY

The blurry line between image and reality has muddied in recent years. What was once editing confined to photoshopped models on magazine covers is now real-life botox and contour makeup on regular old neighborhood moms. What used to be a well-curated work wardrobe that only your coworkers saw is now an endless array of OOTDs on Instagram. (That means Outfit of the Day, for my, ahem, mature readers.)

There was a recent news story lauding Kate Middleton for wearing the same coat twice! A true headliner. A modern heroine. Should we feel vindicated or aghast? I grew up believing people owned exactly one coat that was tied to their identity. "That's Lucy's coat on that chair, so I'm going to sit next to her because she's my friend." Or "Has anyone seen Martin? I think he dropped his coat in the parking lot." How are we supposed to keep up with MULTIPLE coats for ONE person?? It's too much. It's all too much.

Of course image isn't narrowly defined as the representation of oneself in photographs, but for our generation, sharing pictures on social media platforms is undeniably the primary way we present and consume personal presentation. From eyebrow arch to skin clarity to social events and family fun nights, images and 15 second videos are tied together with a cute or clever caption to sum up our lives.

People have tried to impress others since the beginning of time, but only with social media did perfectionism seep into every day moments beyond hosting your in-laws at Christmas or wearing the perfect tea length dress for church each Sunday. The "be yourself" or "keep it real" movement has already exploded to combat the unattainable standards of perfection that social media conjured in the last decade, but even that commendable "natural" movement is tied to image because it's still all about the way we present ourselves. We're supposed to sell ourselves as "honest" vs. "fake." As "vulnerable" vs. "carefree." As "flawed" vs. "manufactured." It's still an image, even if that image aims to loosen the chokehold of perfection.

No matter how long your caption or how "real" your photo, social media and photographs are image-based platforms. They are merely a 2-D representation of who you are. Even if we love fashion or we genuinely enjoy picking out a Halloween group costume (the Leyko *Tiger King* gang was on point in 2020!) or we feel proud of our WOD (Workout Of the Day—I only know this because CrossFit lovers are big sharing types), the truth is that no one can possibly curate a feed that encompasses every aspect of themselves.

When you look around, be it scrolling through Instagram or gawking at the perfectly toned girl in lululemon running down the street, remember what you're doing: You're interpreting an image. You're not actually getting to know a person. You do not know the depth of their struggles. You don't know their reactionary tendencies. You don't know what they think about in the shower or how they treat the plumber. Even if they give glimpses into who they are—perhaps a *lot* of glimpses from naturally open people like me—you absolutely do not know someone until you have a tangible, in-depth relationship with them.

True or false—don't our offline friendships even falter in their transparency?

How often do we *actually* dive into the caverns of our thoughts and dreams with our friends and family? Are we in the habit of vulnerably exposing our fears and insecurities? Who among us naturally peels back the layers of our souls in front of others when we can barely pinpoint them, ourselves? All of that Shrek and Donkey onion business is unnerving. What if someone disagrees with our opinion? What if they aren't capable of a civil debate? What if they think our dreams are frivolous and our fears are indulgent?

Now how much more are we stifled by our fears and privacy when it comes to revealing ourselves to strangers on the internet? Rightfully so! It's a dog-eat-dog world in those comment sections. So if you're mindful of your own exposure, you can be certain everyone else is, too.

See, getting real is a lot harder than posting a few ruminations beneath a selfie with no makeup. Most of the time, we can hardly separate our *own* selves from the image we've created. It takes calculated effort to get to the bottom of who we are instead of living on the surface of who we think we should be. Getting real requires thoughtful assembly of our inner circle, surrounding ourselves with people willing to accept our shaky, ever-shifting souls into their outstretched palms. It requires attracting those sorts of people through reciprocated emotional hospitality. We must allow for conversation and company that challenge our core, bringing forth the person God made before filters and song lyrics and photo-worthy coffee became our identities.

For most of us, part of our deepest self is certainly interwoven with our image. It's okay to share your delicious recipes and handcrafted scrapbooks and philanthropic vacations—our experiences, preferences, and hobbies aren't bad. Makeup isn't evil and smiling for a photo isn't morally corrupt. The challenge here is to avoid letting our image eclipse our truest self. Not only is it impossible to successfully marry the two, but it's dangerous if you begin to think you can.

Same goes for the perception of those around you. Let's not get lost in this assumption that what you see is the whole story.

THE LIKABILITY FACTOR

Imagine a world before "likes" and comment sections, which essentially normalized hot-or-not analytics for our most simple expressions of self. It wasn't too long ago that social media hardly affected our day-to-day, but now pictures are more than a preservation of memories—they're carefully cultivated proof of our worthiness. Some of us are a bit more private than others (I say "us" loosely because I barely fit into the "private" crew—but still, I don't post pictures of my children's poop, so I fall somewhere in the middle), but as a whole, even the most private among us know the feel-good high that accompanies validation in the form of a double tap.

Study after study has proven that seeing a "like" on our posts releases a shot of dopamine into our brains. Just like the snowball of addiction, the more dopamine releases we experience, the more we want. Even a little goody-two-shoes like me who has never once puffed a cigarette or experimented with drugs must recognize and combat the addiction that is image validation. We all know the lengths addicts will go to fuel their craving. Buying followers, timing posts for maximum visibility, deleting posts that don't get enough "likes"—there are endless ways that people are manufacturing validation. Isn't that wild? It's not even legitimate validation that we're looking for. We want the validation of knowing that other people *think* we're validated.

In 2015, Australian Instagram model Essena O'Neill "quit" social media due to the unhealthy pressure to maintain a perfect image. Her story gained traction from *Forbes* to *The New York Times* to CNN, all because she admitted that she went to unreasonable extremes to appear attractive and well liked online. From starving herself for a flatter stomach to spending hours and hours posing to get the perfect angle, berating photographers and family members along the way, Essena eventually realized that none of it was making her happy. So she quit.

In 2014, Penn State freshman and track star Madison Holleran jumped off a seven story parking garage, ending her life after years of feeling inadequate. She saw pictures of her friends having fun and garnering "likes"—even posting happy-go-lucky photos, herself. She knew that her reality didn't stack up to her image, but still assumed everyone else's did. That disconnection left her feeling empty, frustrated, and relentlessly depressed. Her story ended in the worst way imaginable—and she's not the only one.

Now nearly a decade into the Instagram boom, most users are aware that perception of other lives through pictures is hardly a true representation of reality, yet logic still has an uphill battle against that shot of dopamine. We *want* the "likes."

Instagram has toyed with removing “likes” (maybe they’ll be gone by the time this is in your hands), and we applaud it on the outside, but feel tense inside. *How will I know if people think my life is interesting?*

What we present to the world for validation is of equal weight as what we consume. It’s the yin and yang of image. Consuming and sharing spur one another on, creating a cycle of competition, comparison, and fabrication until no one is consuming or sharing anything fully accurate anymore.

Just last week, an acquaintance of mine who I haven’t seen in nearly 15 years messaged me on Instagram about a recipe I’d posted. We got to chatting as we do from time to time because our sons are only a few months apart. Solidarity, sister! A few weeks earlier, she’d mentioned potentially trying for a second child, so I asked her if she’d given that any more thought. Her answer floored me, and broke my heart.

She said that she’d been experiencing panic attacks lately, so she wasn’t sure having another child was the best option. The feelings during these attacks revolved around thinking that her son would be better off without her. She believed she was damaging him emotionally when she’d lose her patience or let her exhaustion rule her emotions.

Postpartum depression isn’t just for brand new mamas. Toddler moms, preschool moms, and kinder-on-up moms are just as susceptible because the pressure never lets up. How can it, with ever-present shining examples of #momlife online?

Guys. I need to say this: Losing patience and being exhausted is normal mom stuff. I'm not encouraging that we yell at our kids or cry in front of them all the time, but my friend thought "good moms" didn't struggle with this sort of thing. So much so that she believed her son would be better off without her! His *mother*! His loving, dedicated mother who adores him so much that she was concerned it wasn't enough! Trust me, it's not the moms who worry about not loving their children enough who aren't loving their children enough.

This isn't the parenting chapter, but her story leads back to image. She admitted that seeing other parents' posts on social media made her believe these lies in her head.

Even my posts. Specifically mine.

Whew, this cut me. I don't feel compelled to swap my cute videos of Anders playing with markers for videos of my hormone-induced rage fits when I peel off the baby carrier (sans baby) like it's strangling me and throw it onto the ground because I'm so frustrated that Jo won't relax in it. *All I wanted to do was take a nice walk with her asleep on my chest GOSHDARNIT!!* I just don't think anyone needs to see that, plus I need to respect my children by not putting our crazy out there.

But ever since that stark and enlightening conversation with my acquaintance, you better believe I try to balance the lot. I use humor so I don't scare anyone, but the message is direct on my social media: This ish is hard.

Dear fellow moms, I am scarring my kids, too, because what kid *hasn't* been scarred by their parents? We can do our absolute best (as we should), but part of our children's inherent beings will be defined by how we as their parents mess up. Best to just accept that now.

My acquaintance let the non-post worthy moments in life eat away at her confidence because she assumed—as we all have at some point—that other people's likable content encompassed their entire existence. That assumption is one of the darkest dangers of our image-driven culture.

Your life is not measured by "likes," followers, comments, filters, or smiling photographs. It's not measured at all! It's just *lived.* It's lived by overcoming your fear of the ocean, running a half marathon, making homemade noodles, getting out of bed after your mom dies, bringing a sick friend soup, or stepping up for people who face oppression. Choose the ingredients to your sense of self wisely because quality ingredients are always tastier than manufactured crap.

Do it to live it, not to post it.

BACK TO BASICS

Researches have sought to determine if social media increases loneliness, or if it does, in fact, provide a sense of community to expel loneliness. Is it actually social, or not?

The results are more interesting than a simple cut and dry, good vs. evil conclusion. Instead of causing or depleting loneliness, turns out social media simply perpetuates whatever end of the scale a person is already on. In other words, if you feel lonely in your day-to-day life, you engage with social media in a way that highlights that loneliness. If you feel relationally fulfilled in your offline life, you experience social media in a way that builds upon that fulfillment.

The lesson here? How we engage (or don't) with people face-to-face is a far stronger force than any community we join online.

Yet even with knowledge of our species' primal need for tangible social intimacy, how many of us spend significantly more time scrolling, posting, assessing, and engaging on social media than building relationships in the same room? Sure, a click of a button feels like a lot less time and effort to get our fix of human "interaction," but is it really?

In 2019, the average person spent 153 minutes per day on social media, or about 2 ½ hours for my mathematically challenged friends out there. That is not insignificant.

In that amount of time, you could engage in five 30-minute phone calls. You could take the A train from Washington Heights down to Hell's Kitchen, walk 10 minutes to Casellula Wine Bar, split a bottle of wine with a friend, and get all the way back home at 181st and Bennett Ave. I would know. I've done that trek at least four dozen times.

Think about it. If we spent even half the amount of time developing our in-person friendships as we do bopping around on Instagram, how would that change our emotional wellbeing? It goes like this: More genuine fulfillment→more positive use of social media→less dependence on "likes"→more genuine connections→more fulfillment.

Healthy relationships on and offline all roll into a snowball that *starts* with our lives *off*line, not the other way around.

A byproduct of investing more energy into our offline relationships is that the stark contrast between reality and image becomes impossible to ignore. We know the ups and downs of our friend's relationships. We see their messy kitchens. We sense their frustration when their kid refuses to eat his peas or gets in trouble for mouthing off in the classroom. We also see the *good* parts that aren't part of a curated image, when somebody gives us a much-needed hug, or makes us laugh with a movie reference. The more we absorb the intricacies that make other humans, well, *human*, the more we are able to recognize that social media image is just one small square in the Rubik's Cube of each individual existence.

DIGITAL ETIQUETTE

I'm just going to cut to the chase: If you're making judgy, rude, or downright nasty comments on someone else's social media page, you are in an unfortunate cycle of loneliness, boredom, and—most likely—personal disdain. Your opinion is completely drowned out by your glaring demonstration of poor character and abundance of time on your hands. You're letting your own shortcomings manifest as criticism, and it's not cute or healthy. I don't care if you see it as a form of entertainment or that public figures "deserve" your opinion—trolling is morally corrupt and downright ineffective.

This kind of angry keyboard trumpeting is what happens when you don't invest in the real-life relationships we just talked about, because only through relational development will you have the depth of experience and wisdom to remember that what you see online is only one dimension of a person. And only with real friendships will you continually hone your face-to-face interpersonal skills that can be transferred to how you speak to someone online.

Kim Kardashian? Melania Trump? Bachelor contestants?

The girl your ex-boyfriend married? They're all human beings. Not every person is morally sound or even respectable, but whatever opinion you have about their decisions isn't going to change a dang thing if it's blasted online in a snarky, malicious, or childish manner. If change is your mission, you're going to need a different approach. If making someone hate themselves is your mission, you're going to need a different heart.

I highly recommend looking up the 9 Elements of Digital Citizenship, which are fundamental and necessary elements of this new online world in which we live. Among those nine principles is *Digital Etiquette: electronic standards of conduct or procedure*. Get this:

As we grow up in schools and homes, we learn basic etiquette both directly and indirectly. For example, your teachers probably taught you not to speak over other people, and your parents probably taught you not to steal food off of someone else's plate without asking. Indirectly, you saw that your parents greeted visitors when they walked into the house or that all of the older students put their trash in the trashcans after eating lunch. From a very young age, we soak in social constructs and civil behavior. It's why we think people on reality TV are trashy for yelling at each other in public restaurants or why we casually say "sorry" when we bump into somebody.

The rub of the 21st century (besides the disappointing irrelevance of the pocket Tamagotchi) is that nobody was taught (or is currently being taught!) guidelines and etiquette when it comes to online interaction. People are making it up as they go, which means they're accidentally warping into strange alien versions of themselves online. I refuse to believe it's just shedding light on how awful most people are. No, instead I think of the internet like tequila—it just brings out the worst in some people, even usually-sane people.

I once heard someone compare our online behavior to that of someone who leaves church and as soon as they're in their car, they flip off other drivers. In different surroundings, every person puts on a new hat. We can hardly help it. Our environment warps our person. This doesn't make someone schizophrenic or deplorable. Maintaining consistency in all of our different environments is shockingly difficult, even if we pride ourselves in personal integrity. The online world is just another environment, and without any formal etiquette or safety training, it's way too easy to develop an altar ego prone to ragey, judgy, self-righteous word vomit.

Generations exposed to social media since grade school are beginning to learn appropriate interactions, but even still, the training is not as formal as many psychologists deem necessary. Though strides are beginning to be made in the message of anti-bullying in online forums, the basic principles of how to convey a message through this new medium are not spelled out. Kids are being told *not* to do something, but aren't being shown how to *do* it.

In my elementary school classrooms, I specifically remember being taught how to write letters. We learned the different greetings based on the formality of who and what we were addressing, proper opening paragraphs, and corresponding signoffs. You don't put "Love, Shannon" when writing to someone you don't know, right? Try "Sincerely" or "Cordially."

The basics of letter etiquette somewhat transferred to e-mail composition, but I was never actually taught the formalities of that medium. I think it's why tone often gets lost in emails—there weren't formal lessons. We're all just winging it, which yields sometimes awkward or unfortunate results. (How many exclamation points is too many?)

Now think about just how different online commentary is from writing a letter. Everybody is just typing whatever comes to mind without any boundaries or notion of appropriate behavior. Kids need to be *taught* how to communicate in this new format!

So do adults. Desperately.

Without the presence of nonverbal communication to steady the wobbly nature of written exchange, and no training on how to handle the absence of such a crucial element of human interaction, the internet has become a divisive world of black and white—everyone firmly on their own side, clinging to whichever army of people agrees with them. And with everyone within screen's reach, it's not hard to find your army.

We are capable of training ourselves on what we failed to learn in grade school. The best place to start your own little curriculum in appropriate interaction on social media? Separate the image that draws out your opinion from the complicated, dynamic, *actual person* behind that image. When you approach the digital world from that headspace, reality and kindness get a much-needed boost, and you'll realize that the headway you want to make in expressing your opinion isn't established through malicious trolling.

AM I THAT VIVACIOUS?

Believe it or not, image issues existed before MySpace. (Is Tom still alive?) Maybe a new wife's mother-in-law expected her to come across classy and put-together, and she felt like she was failing because she wasn't always wearing lipstick or baking a stupid pie. Maybe a man wanted to come across powerful and strong, but struggled with stage fright during company meetings. I mean, these are pretty stereotypical 1950s images, but something tells me they're still not uncommon in today's world. The variations include fashion-lovers needing to make a statement at brunch and carefree crunchy moms ensuring their carts are always full of organic produce.

All of us have an image in our offline lives, like it or not. Wondering what it is? Well, I've come to realize that your image is likely reflective of the three words someone might use to describe you.

In writing this section, I texted three friends to ask them what their words for me would be. I know what my online image is, but it's always interesting to learn what your true real-life image is—and that knowledge is found in how others actually perceive you, not how you perceive yourself.

I'm going to share my own results here, but obviously they are biased toward the positive end of my image since these folks didn't want to offend me. Glad they know I'm a generally fragile person.

Person 1: Loving, vivacious, thoughtful

Person 2: Principled, honest, insightful

Person 3: Passionate, vivacious, loyal

Feeling pretttty good right about now. Two counts for "vivacious"?? Wowza.

I challenge you to ask people in your life to describe you in three words. Do it over a text and call it a personal project so you don't feel as weird. That's what I did. Do it not just for the confidence boost, but so that if there's a word missing of importance to you, you can do some self-reflection.

Without honest feedback of our image, we can't begin the process of improving what we're putting out to the world. For example, I wish that my love for God were more in the forefront of these words. Maybe to replace one of the vivaciouses. Clearly my image doesn't directly point to my faith, and for me, that's troublesome. I want the word "faithful" or "spiritual" to be on the list, so I need to dig deep and figure out why that part of my heart is not an integral part of my image. I don't want to fake it or force it—that's not the point. Rather I want to use the outside to address the inside.

This exercise is also helpful because you'll quickly realize that how you view other people isn't the whole story, just like the words describing you aren't exactly comprehensive. After all, no one described me as hangry or hypersensitive.

Image isn't a bad thing. It's part of you. It can be an exciting form of self-expression or a tool for self-development. Using your image to your advantage, both internally and socially, is far better than letting it simply be an unreliable measure of your worth or confidence. So take control and let it lead you to a life of virtue or consistency or fun pink hair. (Was anyone else tempted to go full Megan Rapinoe after the 2019 World Cup? Just me? Cool.)

CHAPTER 4

health & fitness

HEY GIRL

Let me tell you what makes me burn the hottest. Hotter than when my husband accuses me of understanding the installation process for invisible brackets, meaning it was *inferred* that this "quick" shelving project would take well over *two whole hours*. Hotter than when my yappy little dog pees in the house right after I take her outside. Even hotter than when my son randomly gets Jell-O legs when I'm in a rush trying to put on his dang pants. *Stand up, bud! Just. Stand. Up.*

I *hate*, and I say that in the full sense of the term that requires prayer and repentance, whenever a "Hey girl!" message pops into my message box on Instagram from a complete stranger, asking how I'm doing with "balancing my fitness journey and motherhood."

If you are someone who deploys these tactics, I am not attacking you, personally. I am sure you're a wonderful human who wants to help women live their best lives while making some dough for family vacations. Or whatever. I respect that. I really, really do.

Here's my take, though. If I want your opinion on my body,

how I spend my time and money, and your input of *any* kind on my health, family, or appearance, I will ask. You are not welcome to make implications about my life and priorities simply based on my public photos, or because you've never been formally trained in appropriate and effective sales strategy.

For the love of all things good and holy, do not infer that my butt looks too big by suggesting your virtual boot camp. Do not infer that I look tired by pointing out my need for more "self-care." Self-care is a term that literally makes me want to spend a full 24 hours in a rage room. If you don't know what a rage room is, Google it.

You may be thinking, *Okay Shannon, sounds like you needed to get this rant on paper. But what are we getting at here?* To which I say, you are correct, I *did* need to get that rant on paper. And now for the point: We live in a society that tries to hide its body-obsession (now that it's socially and politically unacceptable to admit you care about physical appearance or size), yet everyone is more body-obsessed than ever. Thus, the new "acceptable" way of selling body-conscious product is to personally bombard people with falsely encouraging words dripping with shame-feeding propaganda. It's all about subtle manipulation.

Fitness empires lead with "self-care." Diet fads lead with "body-love." Everyone is trying to pretend that what they're selling is all about people's happiness, not about people needing to lose weight or capitalizing on people's desire to look good in a swimsuit. Listen, I'm glad sellers are trying to harp on health and confidence instead of bikinis, but let's call a spade a spade. Let's not pretend that "nutrition plans" aren't about weight loss or jean size or making a buck on the natural human desire to feel attractive. Nutrition plan is to diet as scholarship program is to pageant.

I get the point. I really do. I absolutely feel better when my body has more muscle, when I look in the mirror and love the way my shirt hangs, and when I eat a homemade meal that fuels my energy instead of depleting it. Health and happiness through food and fitness is a very real thing. If certain tools or workout regimens help you reach a high level of functionality—use them! However, you must recognize that you will never be fit enough for our society. Your meals will never be healthy enough. Your eyes will never look bright enough. Because if they were, then the health and fitness industry would have nothing left to sell you.

This chapter isn't to pat you on the back and tell you that being 50 or 100 or 200 pounds overweight is A-okay. Sure, that has nothing to do with your worth or your awesomeness, but you and I both know you'd feel a helluva a lot better if climbing the stairs to your second-floor hair salon didn't knock the wind out of you.

This chapter is to underline the importance of leading a physically healthy life while consciously acknowledging that health is not yet another exhausting way you have to keep up with your peers. There will be seasons of strength, and there will be seasons of regression. Sometimes you'll run a turkey trot and pass on the dark meat, and sometimes you'll magically appear in a Taco Bell drive thru and have no idea how in the world you got there. *Darn you, Quesarito sorcery!* Sometimes you'll split an entire package of slice and bake cookies with your husband…every single night of your entire third trimester. And sometimes you'll meal-prep grilled chicken and riced cauliflower religiously for a month until one day a friend's 30th birthday cake sends you back into a week-long spiral of chocolate for breakfast. (I'm not proud.)

Do I believe in health unicorns? That a few #blessed folks are raw carrot lovers and habitual exercisers their entire lives? Yes. Sure. Give them a round of applause! Trust me, they'll get a lot more out of the chapter of this book on home décor or parenthood. *We all have our thing*. But most of us will live in the middle lane of health and fitness, so stop thinking you have to be in the fast lane at all times.

Your marathon-running friend is inspiring, and your church friend who has a bunch of besties from CrossFit have every right to ride those endorphins. It feels good to workout, so let them post the mirror selfie on Instagram! Just keep in mind that whatever way they feel in their bodies has nothing to do with you. Nada. Throw them a "like" for feeling proud about their #mealprep, but separate it entirely from your own self-evaluation.

Give yourself a completely blank slate as you begin to assess what health-oriented routines and results are important to you. Do you care about looking good in shorts? That's legit! Don't go thinking you're shallow for admitting it! Other people couldn't care less about what clothes look like on their body—they just want to be able to carry their giant toddler across a parking lot with ease. Cool! Strength! Love that goal, mama! Does your stomach hurt after you eat dairy? Do you enjoy cooking? Do you prefer chicken or are you more of a bean-eater? Once you start assessing yourself apart from the way health and fitness look on other people—apart from the regimens of random women who flood your inbox with low-key judgmental offers veiled in helpfulness—the sooner you'll stop playing catch-up and start living your most fruitful, energetic life. And I say "fruitful" quite literally. (Ba doom ch!)

MIRROR MIRROR

Does anyone else feel like they don't actually know what they look like? If I try and picture my own face, I truly do not have a clear visual. Is that weird? Am I a ghost?? I just never trust mirrors. I look different in every single one, and I swear every dressing room mirror at Target is tilted at a different angle. Sometimes I'm killing the game, and sometimes I do not recognize the beast in front of me.

Even though our reflections are never the same, and we'll never get a true, direct look at ourselves the way other people see us (isn't that trippy to think about??), mirrors are usually the catalyst for whatever feelings we have about our bodies.

In some ways, I hope the mirror is the catalyst for healthy habits rather than a heart attack or the inability to run a mile. Your reflection is allowed to be a catalyst for a change in how you take care of yourself, but it's *not* allowed to be a catalyst for how you determine your worth.

Here, let me put the words in a different order just in case it didn't resonate the first time:

A mirror is not allowed to determine your worth.

Do you get that? Do not let it cross that line. Tell that mirror to get back in its place along with your overbearing coworker and all the guys from Hannah Brown's season of *The Bachelorette*.

Stay in your lane, Mirror. Your lane involves telling me if my outfit clashes, if I have toothpaste on my chin, or if there's a bad guy standing behind me with a scary slasher knife. You may also remind me that my heart can't handle all of the cheeseburgers I ate during the first trimester, so I should maybe lay off the grease. However, cheeseburgers in my middle section have nothing to do with my lovability, intelligence, personality, or right to belong to a community. Also, you're just a mirror. You have the audacity to think you control me?? Nah, humans trump mirrors. I win. Sorry, bud.

Listen, I don't really subscribe to this popular practice of looking in the mirror and telling yourself that you're gorgeous no matter what you see. I'm not afraid to admit that I'm not all that physically appealing when I have mascara under my eyes and a few zits on my chin in the morning. Why is it so bad to admit that not every part of humanity is super alluring? Who freaking cares if you're not always the hottest thing that ever walked into Safeway? Does it really matter? No! I do ask that you don't wear pajama pants to the grocery store, but if you're afraid to grab some milk without first applying eyeliner, we need to have a talk.

Feeling pretty all the time shouldn't be the goal. You are not always beautiful. Sorry to be the bearer of bad news, but it's true. Even genetic masterpieces like Mila Kunis have looked rough before. The sooner you accept your not-so-appealing moments, the sooner you can genuinely accept your whole self. The goal isn't about attaining beauty or convincing yourself that you are gorgeous. I mean, yes, I deeply believe that all humans are made by God and are therefore absolutely stunning—truly, I believe that—but I just don't believe that's the goal when it comes to appreciating ourselves. The *goal* is to develop confidence in all the good stuff beneath the surface. The soul-part that soars up to heaven, not what rots in the ground.

That way, on mornings you wake up looking like Shrek, or for those few postpartum years which result in 24/7 BO and all kinds of weird-looking marks on your stretched-out wannabe Elastigirl body, you can still love who you are. And not in the I'm-convincing-myself-to-love-me way. I want you to barely flinch when your face resembles a pizza and your hair breaks itself into makeshift bangs. (Again, postpartum is fun.)

The key here is realism. You don't need to love the stretch marks. Society tells you you're supposed to because of what they represent, but if you can't make yourself swoon over purple scars and wrinkly skin, you're not crazy. Adopting all the feel-good mumbo jumbo is a whole lot of work considering your confidence has nothing to do with whether or not you sincerely adore your stretch marks. If you prescribe to said mumbo-jumbo and it's working for you, then keep taking that pill girlfriend, because you're gorgeous! For the rest of us who aren't really turned on by our rosacea and cellulite, it's time to strive for a confidence that stems from a self-love that can withstand a button popping off your jeans on a day you forget to say your morning affirmations.

Body image issues affect 80-90% of the female population, depending on which study you reference—and believe me, I've referenced many. That's a heck of a lot of body insecurities. Just because I'm telling you not to attach your worth to the mirror doesn't negate the fact that most of us struggle with liking the way we look.

But I have a solution: The best way to take the focus off the mirror and start processing your worth in relation to your soul—your spirit that inhabits the shell that carries it—is to lean into the areas of your life that feed your natural talents. Does writing bring you clarity? Are your witty comments stinkin' hilarious? Are you good at organizing birthday celebrations for your office? Does your brain crunch numbers like a human calculator? Do you give really legit momming advice? Do you pray earnestly for specific people every night? Think about the things you love to do that are a result of your own unique gifts and goodness. Isn't that awesome?? How great is your existence??

Once you start filling your time with the things that make you happy to be you, the less the physical vessel that carries all those gifts and goodness will be a determining factor in how much you like yourself. Instead, you can start seeing your physical form as a necessary transportation system. It's through that lens that you crack down on your health or shave your legs. What you bring to the table is needed, so it would be a real travesty for you to keel over or smell too gross to be of help to people who have questions about taxes or baby poop or whatever you're good at handling. Let's make sure your heart is healthy enough to enjoy advice sessions with a glass of wine, or your hair is brushed so that people in the office enjoy your cake without wondering if it's safe to eat because of your personal hygiene.

The less we focus on something, the less it matters. Don't water what you don't want to grow. Modern self-love is a lot like someone telling you to not think of a blue elephant. What are you thinking of right now? Bluey the blue blue elephant. Of course we shouldn't brush body image issues under the rug, but if you give your energy and ultimate merit to completely different areas of yourself and your life, your body's shape becomes way less of a concern.

ONE SIZE DOES NOT FIT ALL

Anyone who has watched Serena Williams play tennis and also watched Meryl Davis ice dance knows that weight can vary drastically among extremely fit people.

I used to compete in the Miss America Organization back when there was a swimsuit portion of competition called "Lifestyle & Fitness," but we all just called it Swimsuit because pageant people are surprisingly un-PC in nature. Outside of Pageant World (where pale skin and carbs go to die), the general public saw Swimsuit as antiquated and vulgar. Inside Pageant World, no one cared all that much about the feminist complaints. Instead, the drama surrounding Swimsuit was whether or not judges should be looking for true fitness or simply someone who was lean. I regret to inform you that most of the time, these two categories did not intersect.

Nine times out of 10, the girl who won Swimsuit would be one of the skinniest girls competing. Meanwhile, the women with big leg muscles and six packs would be labeled "too masculine." *We want long and lean muscles, ladies! Don't bulk up!* This singular definition of "fit" was a hot debate among competitors (and their very involved mothers) because why call it "Lifestyle & Fitness" if it's really just about who can crash diet most successfully right before the big day?

Unfortunately, this same sort of one-type-fits-all standard for fitness doesn't only rear its head while wearing a tiara. It's no secret that for decades, women have been expected to wear a size 2-4 alongside a myriad of other physical banners of excellence. Tina Fey said it best:

> ...I think the first real change in women's body image came when JLo turned it butt-style. That was the first time that having a large-scale situation in the back was part of mainstream American beauty. Girls wanted butts now. Men were free to admit that they had always enjoyed them. And then, what felt like moments later, boom—Beyoncé brought the leg meat. A back porch and thick muscular legs were now widely admired. And from that day forward, women embraced their diversity and realized that all shapes and sizes are beautiful.
>
> Ah ha ha. No. I'm totally messing with you. All Beyoncé and JLo have done is add to the laundry list of attributes women must have to qualify as beautiful. Now every girl is expected to have Caucasian blue eyes, full Spanish lips, a classic button nose, hairless Asian skin with a California tan, a Jamaican dance hall ass, long Swedish legs, small Japanese feet, the abs of a lesbian gym owner, the hips of a nine-year-old boy, the arms of Michelle Obama, and doll

> tits. The person closest to actually achieving this look is Kim Kardashian, who, as we know, was made by Russian scientists to sabotage our athletes.

So good.

To swing it back toward the bucket of health, correlating weight with fitness is so twisted it's not even funny. Unless Tina Fey makes it funny. Sure, medical research proves that excess weight or lack of necessary weight are absolutely linked to health issues. That's just a fact. You can love yourself at every shape and size, but you can't get around the fact that your arteries must be clear for you receive oxygen and survive. It's no wonder weight is such a hot topic when nearly half of our country's citizens—39.8% to be precise—are obese. Couple that statistic with the cultural standard of beauty (even plus size models should have a sharp jawline!), and we shouldn't be surprised to find ourselves bombarded with proclamations and products all revolving around the size of our pants.

Because beauty standards have become so muddled with fitness and health, it feels almost offensive to fall into the "unhealthy" category. Maybe we can't tie our shoes or carry the car seat easily, but if someone—even a doctor—points out inadvertently or God forbid blatantly that we're not our healthiest self, we hear "ugly." "Worthless." "Judged." I mean, hi! That's exactly what I hear when those Hey Girls slide into my DMs with workout offers. (Except instead of feeling bad about myself, I just get really angry because my genes gave me a temper. My jeans actually do, too, sometimes.)

Creating a distinction between the words "health" and "beauty" gives you the freedom to address the necessity of the first without stumbling on the arbitrary, unattainable nature of the second. Join me in drawing this line.

Say it with me: Everybody is different. In many aspects of life, including health and fitness, our journeys will be distinct and our finish lines will be unique. The scales will say a different number, the curves in our bodies will swoosh and straighten at different angles, and what mentally serves one person well will not serve another. Give yourself the discipline to improve your health in a way that is not simply measured by weight, and the grace to embrace your body's uniquely fierce manifestation of strength.

Although after two kids, I don't mind the thought of those doll tits Tina jokes about.

IS BUTTER A CARB?

Anyone on a Keto or Whole 30 diet is going to tense up when they read this, but here's the skinny (no pun intended): Fad diets of today are equivalent to fads like South Beach and Atkins of yesteryear. Consumers have become more averse to certain ad language and more privy to nutritional value, but that doesn't mean fad diets aren't exactly what they are. Though modern advertising now calls them a "lifestyle choice," don't be fooled by Don Draper! They're still regimented ways of eating that ultimately focus on losing weight or maintaining a certain physique.

This isn't to say all fad diets are unhealthy. Is the no-sugar, no-dairy formula of Whole 30 bad for your body? Probably not! Is eating more veggies and fewer noodles better for you? I mean, I wouldn't know first-hand. Pasta is life. Can't stop won't stop. But it's probably safe to say that the vitamins and minerals (I still speak like I'm in 5th grade health class) found in veggies will give you more energy and less cellulite than fettuccini Alfredo. Such a buzz kill! Legitimate healthiness aside, whether you only eat red meat or swear off everything but tofu and cauliflower—if you're following a regimented diet created by someone else who profits off of the trademark, then I have some news for you my friend: You are on a fad diet.

Weight loss is a $66 billion, yes billion, dollar industry as of 2018. If you think all of those dollar bills are wrapped up in good intentions, you are optimistic and I applaud your high spirits. As for critics like me, we note that repeat customers are a pretty massive chunk of that staggering profit, and therefore call into question if these diets ever really work. And what does "working" even mean?

According to Health Research Funding, more than 95% of people will relapse from a diet in five years or less. Frankly, I don't know how anyone even gets to the one year mark with no chocolate or carbs, so color me impressed by anyone who reaches a full five years before backsliding. Still, this rinse and repeat cycle tells me that diets are mostly about wrestling yourself into submission, eventually losing the brawl.

It's hard to be truly healthy when you're miserable. And when you're miserable, you make more unhealthy choices. The snowball of all snowballs. Or the meatball of meatballs..? (I'll be here all night, folks!)

If you want some structure in your diet in order to fight off the temptation to go buck wild, I applaud seeking out a formulated plan that gets you excited. What I want you to know before going into it, though, is that you're not a worthless bump on a log if you have a hard time sticking to it or gain back the weight. Healthy eating is hard when the grocery store offers

87 different flavors of potato chips and that dang bag of double dark chocolate Milanos stares you down from the checkout line. Structure can be a great tool to ward off health threats, but you're not the only one who's ever been defeated by the buffet of packaged bait lining the exit aisle.

The overarching goal is to see food as fuel. Enjoyable fuel! Once you stop seeing food as this thing you have to control or manage, then your choices will begin to look a little more moderate and a little less…faddy. (See what I did there? Faddy? Fatty? I'm proud. Not deleting.)

THE FOUNDATION FOR EVERYTHING

From Barack Obama to Warren Buffet, an astonishing number of high-profile individuals who've reached the top of their fields attribute their success to a dedication to health and fitness. Obama noted that he was unmotivated professionally until he began running three miles a day. In an essay for the book *Getting There*, Warren Buffet emphasizes caring for your body as you would an expensive car.

When we're tempted to measure our fitness in terms of discretionary beauty, we lose sight of the *why*. Not the "I want to look sexy in a dress" *why*, but the *why* that shapes our dreams, our purpose, and our impact. The *why* that carried these and other powerful people to their influential seats at the table.

We all want to be great at something, right? Even if you don't want to become President of the United States (my personal nightmare) or a renowned investor like the leaders referenced above, you still have hopes for your life. Being an extraordinary parent, writing a book, landing a Broadway gig, becoming a missionary, learning to play guitar, moving up the promotional ladder—whatever you dream of for your life—that's your *why*.

If you want to achieve anything at all, you must start by taking care of the foundation: Your existence, itself.

Even if your brand of greatness has nothing to do with being physically fit, your brain is connected to your body, and you *must* pay attention to those synapses. It could be meditation, yoga, running, or rec league dodge ball. The point is to engage our bodies, because they are irrevocably entwined with our minds.

When I was 10 years old, being the manipulative child I was, I told my mom that the reason I couldn't do my homework was because I was unable to concentrate.

"It's probably ADHD," I proclaimed, proudly aware of a medical condition recently assigned to a few of my classmates.

My mother, being the type of woman and R.N. she was, told me to go run a mile in our neighborhood, then come back and see if I could do my homework. *Welp, that backfired, Shannon.*

I mean, it was slightly ballsy of my mom to not believe me considering one time I complained that I hurt my wrist while roller blading, and she refused to take me to a doctor for a full 24 hours only to find out that I'd broken it in two places and fractured it in three. Or that other time that I grumbled about how my theatre teacher was irrational for claiming the audience could see details of our faces on stage for a full year before we discovered I was blind as a bat.

Alas, I didn't have ADHD. I ran a mile and begrudgingly completed my math assignment.

ADHD specialist Kerri Golding wrote, "Exercise not only encourages the production of dopamine, norepinephrine, and serotonin in the brain, but by doing so has the same effect on the brain as the stimulant methylphenidate (Ritalin)." Basically, exercise might be just as effective as a focus-enhancing drug.*

Ugh, why are our moms always right? (Wait, will this eventually become true for my kids too…?)

*It's important to note that I am not a doctor, and that I also fully trust that many people require medication. I'm just saying that going for a jog won't hurt the cause.

SMOKE & MIRRORS

To reiterate, friends, please don't believe what you see on social media. Despite the amount of meal prep and gym selfies flooding your newsfeed, 90% of adults in the United States fail to eat the recommended amount of fruits and veggies per day. And while one survey claimed that 74% of Americans workout one or more days a week, another study found that only 18% of Americans have a gym membership. I'm going to put my Inspector Gadget childhood to good use here and assume that quite a few people were lying on that survey about working out weekly. Something tells me that the 56% gap is too wide to be accurate. Not *that* many people who are dedicated to working out don't have a gym membership.

I'm also fortunate to have a large circle of friends whose lives I'm privy to witnessing offline, and I can tell you that for every gym selfie, there are days, weeks, and months of no fitness regimen in sight. So even the folks who do have gym memberships don't tend to use them super regularly year round. Some do, which is fabulous for them. And some work out weekly without a gym membership, but let's not put undue faith in what we're comparing ourselves to online.

Not only are people not working out or eating as well as it looks in their #mealprep pictures and gym posts, but a million other reasons aside from healthy choices can alter someone's appearance. And I'm not talking about FaceTune (please don't). I'm talking about stress.

When people are going through a particularly difficult time in their lives, their bodies react in different ways. Some folks gain weight, because stress releases cortisol into our systems, which is a hormone that contributes to belly fat. Others lose their desire to eat entirely. After my mother passed away from bladder cancer, I lost 10 pounds. When my friend's father passed away unexpectedly, she gained 30 pounds.

Imagine how many people in similar situations never admit that their fitness or weight journeys have very little to do with their actual wellbeing? Maybe they're going through something deeply upsetting. Maybe they're using diet pills, purging, or starving themselves. What people tell you—or even show you—about their health and what they're actually experiencing are often two vastly different things.

Are you sensing a theme yet? Comparison is poison.

TRUE HEALTH

Our legitimate health is measured by, yes, our vitals at the doctor's office, but also by our relationships, gratitude, personal drive, and interactions with the world around us. To be healthy is to be truly alive. You are already here, so you might as well come alive! Your mere presence on this earth is an opportunity to experience the depth of joy through pursuing health in its most undiluted form. This requires more than vegetables. More, even, than a glowing report from the doctor.

The word "health" is diminished in its importance when we limit its association to just our bodies. Our bodies will all change and become less "ideal" simply because Benjamin Button Syndrome is not a real thing. Botox or not, you will get older, break a bone, push out a baby, tweak your back when putting on your shoes, develop weird veins, and your bottom teeth will shift. While I obviously support reaching a place of physical wellbeing, I don't think enough people sit back and truly come to terms with how our abilities and appearance inevitably change with age. You cannot escape the fact that your body's shape, how much you can lift, or how fast you can run will all change. Your body in its "prime" is fleeting, and we're chasing ghosts in the attempt to what—become Voldemort? That's not even cute, guys.

The only part of your physicality that matters is how it paves the way for more confidence, relationships, drive, spirituality, and self-esteem. In order to develop positive habits and fulfillment in those areas, your body must be a willing and able partner. *That* is the worth of physical health.

But the areas of fulfillment it supports are the only determining factors of true health.

CHAPTER 5
parenthood

HAVING CHILDREN ISN'T NEW

Offspring are required for the survival of our species. Our bodies are constantly looking for opportunities to preserve their legacies.

Why are bars full of guys in shirts that are just a smidge too tight and girls wearing heels that they secretly hate but claim make them feel powerful (i.e. their legs look longer)? Because *babies*. It's all because *babies*.

Some folks may not consciously want kids—or be driven by the possibility of having kids for a whole boatload of reasons (sexual orientation, medical diagnoses, and enjoyment of quietly eating at restaurants come to mind)—but I'm here to tell you that the reason we desire affection is more than just the basic need for human touch and intimacy. It's because BABIES.

Enjoying sex for pleasure is totally legit. And that's a great thing. I believe it's entirely intended for pleasure to be the conscious motivation to do the dirty. Still, a 2015 study named "Sexual selection protects against extinction" dives into this reality: Somewhere deep down in our biological makeup is a cape-flying hero of mankind, set out on the mission to save the future of humanity from going extinct through a whole lot of sexy time.

This isn't the parenting chapter you thought it'd be, is it? Don't worry, it is. I'm just starting at the very beginning, which is a very good place to start. So Julie Andrews once told me.

The birds and the bees lead to these adorable crying blobs of mush that slowly, yet remarkably and sometimes devastatingly, turn into you and me: More humans who like sex, companionship, and stability.

For those of us who one day find ourselves pushing a watermelon-sized creature out of our lady parts, or those of us who adopt and foster munchkins that don't care if you share DNA as long as you give them goldfish and Elmo, well—we're a crazy, competitive, motley crew called parents. All we're doing is the same thing that literally every generation has done before us (congrats, heroes, for we are not yet extinct!), yet we think we must reinvent the wheel or that we are colossally messing it all up.

We need more wine.

Before parenting blogs and WebMD and organic lunchbox kits, there were just a bunch of people having sex and making babies. They put food in those babies' mouths, told them not to shove their siblings, and explained that in order to get an A on their next test, they'd have to study harder.

This newly developed dedication to unofficial internet education, online mommy groups, and don't-let-them-struggle parenting is not only exhausting, but harmful. Yes, harmful to the kids, but also destructive to the ones causing the mess in the first place: Parents. All of a sudden we have access to studies (or at least interpretations of studies sprinkled with bias) and examples of other families on social media, so it's the perfect parenting storm. Matching Christmas jammies, toned post-partum buttocks, gentle-well-researched discipline, and masterful first grade projects have become an impenetrable gold standard even though we all know it's completely unrealistic.

We *know* that no parent has ever survived toddlerhood or tweenhood without raising their voice at least one time, and yet we are filled with despair when it's our turn to accidentally lose our mind in front of our child. Despite our logical side reminding us that parenting doesn't come with a scorecard, we somehow think we can implement everything we've ever read, keep the schedules, get the kids in the matching pajamas, force the carrots, and nail the homework.

We fight for our child's top-of-class status, bartering for extensions and undermining teachers. We brag about our 18-month-old knowing all his colors. We cook food blogger recipes and can tell you every single benefit of breastfeeding. We take dreamy family photos in local wheat fields, manage 70 extracurricular activities, and FaceTime Grandma at least once a week. We spend our time at work guilty and our time at home resentful.

Guys. Stop being crazy. Stop convincing yourself that you've done something wrong because your toddler bit a kid at school. Oh my gosh, we *know* you're not sitting at home teaching him how to sink his teeth in! It just happens. (At least that's what Anders' patient teachers told me when I started crying after he repeatedly tried to devour one of his classmates.) Stop being holier-than-thou because your kid sleeps well, while simultaneously crying in the shower because you can't afford Insta-worthy birthday gifts this year. Stop the madness!

Loving our children can push us to behave in wild, mama-bear ways. In many regards, that is commendable, instinctual, and so very sweet. But please, for the love of boxed mac and cheese, occasionally choose a little instinct over internet. We've got to stop creating fragile humans because we forget that pain is part of growth. We've got to stop agreeing to the wrapping paper fundraiser and signing up for the church potluck when what we truly need to do is take a nap.

THE CIVIL WAR

The division between mothers who "have their own identity" and those who are "defined by their kids" is usually a battle between working moms (WMs) and stay-at-home moms (SAHMs).

I've been both. I worked full time during my first year of motherhood, at one point bringing my newborn with me to the office. Then I became a SAHM when he was 17 months (pregnant with Baby #2). From firsthand experience, I can tell you that one is not better than the other. One is not easier or does not make someone stronger. They're different experiences, each with legitimate difficulties and undeniable perks. On one side of the coin, you get to pee in privacy (WM), and on the other, you have easy access to chocolate ice cream in your refrigerator whenever you please (SAHM). Different types of blessings.

Unfortunately, moms justify their decision or circumstance to stay at home or go to work, then sneak attack the other "side" with loaded Facebook statuses or Instagram quotes.

[A few of the] Justifications of Working Moms:

"I want my kids to grow up seeing that women can do it all, and that they have a strong, capable mommy."

"I think it's important to contribute to our family financially."

"I don't want to be one of those moms who loses her identity in her kids. I need the stimulation."

[A few of the] Justifications of Stay-At-Home Moms:

"I don't want someone else to raise my children."

"I made the choice to put my children first, before my career or anything else."

"I believe I was made to be a mother."

Now take a look at those justifications, and glean the implications. Working moms make stay-at-home moms feel inferior. That they are somehow less capable and strong. Spoiled. Lost. Mundane. Stupid. Too comfortable.

Stay-at-home moms make working moms feel guilty. That they are less devoted to their kids. Selfish. Lacking the innate ability to mother whole-heartedly.

Even backhanded compliments between SAHMs and WMs add fuel to this war of justifications:

"Oh I could NEVER stay at home with the kids! I'd go crazy. I don't know how you do it."

"Oh I could NEVER go to work every day and manage my guilt. You're stronger than I am!"

What each side is actually saying is "I'm too intelligent to do what you're doing," or "I'm too loving to do what you're doing."

Recognizing differences would be to genuinely respect the other side of the coin. To be intentional with how your words—even thoughts—might implicate another mom who has a completely different set of worldviews. For example, if you say, "I only get two hours with my kids each night, so I am more focused and dedicated during my time with them," are you watering down the ample time another person has? I don't advocate for walking on eggshells, though if that's how you have to start in order to create a new way of thinking and communicating, then maybe a few eggshells are in order. We must break down the defensive, justified walls that mothers build in pursuit of raising these little munchkins we love so fiercely.

Now, these justifications often come from necessity, right? Most WMs or SAHMs don't have a choice. Most mothers are working or not working based on the financial gain of their household—they either need a second income, or the cost of childcare outweighs the point of having two working parents. And while I'd love to use this moment to point out how lopsided, sexist, and oppressive it is that women are usually expected to be the ones to quit and stay home—even if she enjoys working—I think we all already know that's a major issue. So I'll try to focus on the point at hand: It's not that justifications are a bad thing, necessarily. If something is not a choice, it's a good survival tactic to find positivity in your circumstance. And if something *is* a choice, it's good to believe you made the best one…or else what are you doing?

The problem with justification is forgetting—as we often do—that people are not the same. Your personal justification should have no bearing on the way you see another mom's decision, *or on the way you make them feel*, even inadvertently.

Perspectives are not the same. Needs, desires, types of intelligence, love languages, relationships, and purposes are not the same. And no, backhanded compliments do not count as being "nonjudgmental." Telling someone that their choice would be too hard for you is *not* humbly recognizing differences.

I've personally doled out justifications and backhanded compliments while working, before staying at home. I regret saying them—even thinking them. I know they didn't come from a place of judgment, but ultimately, that's what they are. I can now see that truth more clearly having lived a little on both sides of the coin. Since I've chosen to no longer justify either experience to myself—rather I'm open to ping-ponging between being a WM and a SAHM as life unfolds—I'm more objectively observant of this divide between WMs and SAHMs. I've felt the brunt of judgment on both ends, and have landed in a place of near-disinterest in the debate altogether. Frankly, after all my contemplation, I hardly see a difference between my choice or circumstance to be a SAHM vs. a WM.

At the end of the day, I love my children the exact same amount. I do my best with the time I have with them, whether it's two hours a day or 24. I know that whatever they experience as a result of me working or not working is in God's hands, anyway. After all, we all know well-adjusted, happy individuals who spent their childhood in daycare or those who spent their childhood at home.

If we love our children whole-heartedly, then as moms, all of our decisions are equally "right"…unless you're letting your toddler run next to a cliff or are too disengaged to stop your kid from bullying classmates. In that case, get it together, lady.

THE SOCIAL SHIFT

Those of you living the Single Income No Kids (SINK) life and the Dual Income No Kids (DINK) life have a whole different set of challenges when it comes to how you define yourself within the kid stratosphere, despite not having kids. The fact that the terms SINK and DINK even exist goes to show that no matter who we are in adulthood, we're categorized by having or not having children.

This needs to be said: Not having children is no better or worse than having them. Period. If you do not have children either by choice or infertility, you are no less blessed or strong, no more selfish or sophisticated. Children are a unique experience in life that can bring about an extraordinary amount of love and growth, but they are not the only experience in life that can produce wisdom, purpose, and unconditional love. If your story doesn't involve parenting, I promise that it involves pouring into this world in a way that parents simply cannot. SINKs and DINKs are a necessary balance in our communities, even if it means there's a sharp difference in how they vacation. As in, they can actually relax.

It's impossible to ignore the lifestyle differences between parents and non-parents, often leading to a more challenging dynamic in developing or maintaining friendships. This isn't to say parents and non-parents cannot become or remain friends, but if someone's daily life revolves around diapers and scraping full jars of blue agave off the floor (if that seems oddly specific, let me just say that last night was eventful for the Leyko family), then happy hour or birthday dinners probably aren't in the cards. Babysitters are expensive. Personal energy is even more expensive. Mama's *poor*, y'all.

Side note: Trust me when I say it's far more stressful for the parents with rambunctious children in public places than it is annoying for you. Cut them some slack and buy them a drink.

Some SINKs and DINKs are entirely comfortable with kid-friendly locations, or being the ones to come over instead of host (parents would much rather their children mess up their own house than yours, just FYI). But that kind of awareness and effort doesn't always come naturally when you're used to carefree social environments where you can sit in one place for more than 30 seconds without compromising the safety of a small human life. I appreciate non-parents who realize they have more flexibility to make the bigger effort, but I certainly don't blame them for becoming disenchanted. It's hard to remain day-in, day-out friends when there's a basic lack of true understanding in shared experience, or when imbalance of resources and time threatens the equilibrium.

Friendships are about supporting one another, and sometimes

that capacity for support changes, depletes, or strengthens in waves throughout your life. Always keep an open heart toward those from whom you've drifted because they might become pillars again as your lives realign down the road. Just don't be surprised (or offended) if the childrearing years adjust your circle. At least until the kids can wipe their own butts.

GETTING ANTSY

Reasons for falling into the SINK or DINK category differ, but more often than not, SINKs (reminder: S for Single Income—usually single relationally, as well) simply haven't reached the point in their lives where they're settled down and ready for kids. Traditionally, finding a mate is the first part of the family equation, so waiting on that type of relationship to come to fruition is the most common reason SINKs do not have spawn. (I love calling my kids "spawn.")

At some point, your friends begin marrying off, either staying DINKs (reminder: Dual Income) for a while or starting to pop out children. You find yourself more and more annoyed with the endless weddings and baby showers (your bank account is probably even more annoyed), and you begin feeling left behind. At first, you felt bad for your friend who can no longer sleep past 7 a.m., but then suddenly you realize you're the only one still sleeping until 10, and that makes you kind of antsy.

Not only are you waiting (im)patiently for your love timeline to get on track, but you're also beginning to get those awkward remarks about your biological clock during Thanksgiving dinner.

To top it off, you're finding it harder and harder to relate to your friends whose kids are now the center of their lives. Even if you love being single, there's no doubt that at some point it can feel like you're missing out, which tends to manifest as self-pity or defensive judgment:

I mean, I thought she didn't even like babies all that much. Now she won't post a single picture on Instagram that isn't of her infant. And I swear if I hear one more thing about potty training, I'm defriending her. Doesn't she have anything to do other than talk about her kids?

Listen, I can't fully explain exactly why new parents feel this unmanageable urge to share photos of their kids and openly talk about their baby's poop, but it's a serious magnetic pull. We can't help it. Please forgive us.

It's easy to see these babies magically appear and spread like wildfire on your timeline, as though every woman from your high school had a secret group text and decided together to start churning out the next gen. Not only that, but did they have a naming party? Because there seem to be only three categories: Names that end in "lyn," names that sound like whimsical characters from a time travel novel (Finn, Ava, River, etc.), or the mother's maiden name. In all fairness, my maiden name was Oliver, which was one glass of champagne away from becoming my son's name, but then I learned he'd be the fifth Oliver in each of his classrooms growing up (Oliver also falls into the time travel category), so we went with one of the most common names in Sweden instead. Anders! Hard A. Short for Anderson, which—you guessed it—was a surname in my family tree. Couldn't help myself. I'm telling you, these three millennial naming categories are hard to resist.

Given that your entire peer group was apparently texting without you, you might suddenly feel ashamed of your SINK status. Maybe you should join Match instead of Tinder, because that feels more serious, right? *In order to have kids and join the secret mom society, I better find me a man.*

Screeeeech! Pump the breaks, sister.

This is the part where I beg you not to get married just because you want babies. I mean, I definitely recommend finding a partner first because trust me when I say that the infant stage is not a one-woman job (though ridiculously huge props to single parents—you are true warriors and time and time again, I've seen you provide more love and stability than plenty of two parent homes), but attaching yourself to a mate solely for reproductive circumstances is not a grand idea for a happy, healthy life.

Despite the freshness rating of your eggs, the baby fever you feel when holding a newborn, or the desire to once again be able to relate to your friends, marriage must be based on all the things that will exist *before and after* children: love, compatibility, trust, commitment, and a mutual love for Mexican food. (See Chapter 1!)

If your reason for falling in the SINK (I'm punny!) is that you haven't found a partner with whom you want to reproduce, remind your ovaries that the odds are in your favor to eventually meet the right person. You can even freeze your eggs if you use *Bachelor* contestant discount codes at their recommended clinics. (This is not a drill.) Broadway star Audra McDonald conceived a baby the old-fashioned way when she was 45 years old, and continued full-out dancing in her show *Shuffle Along* during her pregnancy, which ironically sounds like it could have been the title to my last pregnancy, as well.

While Audra is, in fact, a human anomaly in both talent and grace—a description to which I can personally attest since I was a server during her pre-show opening night soiree for *Porgy and Bess*, and at the time I was 23 and idiotic, so I didn't recognize her and offered her champagne not once, but three times before she kindly told me she couldn't drink before [starring in] the show—she is also an inspiring example that your biological clock might work just fine even if you push snooze a few times. Even if it doesn't, it's not worth risking the pitfalls of an unhealthy marriage. If that's the route you're contemplating, just Andy Cohen or Kristin Davis the whole thing and fly solo. It's hard to be a single parent, but harder still to parent with the emotional burden of a floundering partnership.

INFERTILITY & DISRUPTION

When I miscarried my second child around eight weeks into my pregnancy, I wasn't surprised. I woke up to find some spotting, but tried to tell myself that sometimes women lightly bleed during the first trimester, so I headed to the office for a normal day of work. By midday, it was more than spotting, and I knew exactly what was going on. I cried as I drove myself to the emergency room, wondering if it was even a necessary step in the process, but figured I could use some form of medical closure.

During that drive, watching cars zip past and wondering if anyone else was suffering behind their moving metal walls, I tried to figure out what I felt. My tears confirmed I was sad. My heart confirmed I was grieving. But my brain somehow told me it was fine. I'd already seen this coming. I prepared for this back when I learned that 1 in 5 pregnancies end in miscarriage. When three of my close friends lost their unborn babies back to back.

In the weeks that followed, during the awkward and emotionally painful experience of continuing to physically miscarry onto a giant maxi pad for a days on end, I kept staring at my then 10-month-old son. I already had one perfect, squishy child.

My heart knew to be grateful, and I was. I really did trust God's will, perhaps an easier task for me than others because I had my son or because I was experienced in faith through trauma after losing my mother. Being grateful didn't cancel out the legitimacy of my grief, but it sure helped.

Instead of focusing on my pain, I decided to arm myself with information. I began researching secondary infertility, which is the inability to conceive or carry after successfully carrying another child. Apparently 30% of infertility cases are secondary, meaning that the whole "you've done it once and can do it again" adage is a pretty hefty misnomer. And, by the way, a damaging phrase to recite to women who desire more children, but may not be able to have them.

A girlfriend of mine had three consecutive miscarriages between her two living children. Another had two second-trimester stillbirths in the *same year*, but years prior, had two healthy pregnancies and deliveries. Through research and observation, I've come to realize just how many women feel behind in life because their bodies don't cooperate. It's painful to feel so out of control over something of such magnitude. The desire for children isn't something you can shake off or simply spin for the positive. That hole is deep. It's biological, spiritual, and physical.

During my own brush with infertility, my coping mechanism was to keep moving. Classic doer. So I Googled adoption.

Adoption has been part of my plan since I was in elementary school. I had no idea how reproduction worked or anything about starting a family, but my soul was loud and clear: *Shannon, you are going to adopt.*

I think a lot of factors led to this innate knowing. I grew up in a very interracial church, surrounded by diverse friends as a Navy Brat, traveled to India twice in my teens to volunteer at AIDS and tsunami relief orphanages, and became best friends (still am) with a girl who was adopted, herself. My want to adopt didn't revolve just around race, but I do think it started there. White saviors are a thing, and before educating myself on that very real principle, I accidentally found myself inside that echoey well. My intentions were good, but we all know the road those pave.

By college, I'd done enough research about adoption to reevaluate my heart and even learn the term "white savior," which requires constant education and evaluation even to this day. I'm not saving a child. I'm not providing a "better life" for a child. I am simply loving a child, as all children deserve to be. I am mothering a child. The line can feel blurry, but boy is it important to stay on the correct side of it.

After my failed pregnancy, Aaron and I decided that perhaps it was time to get more serious about our intent to adopt. It was always Plan A, but when's the right time, you know?

Well, a month after finding an agency we were interested in using, I wound up pregnant again. This time with our daughter, Jo. Still, not three months after she was born, I was knee-deep back in the adoption waters.

At first glance, adoption feels like a guaranteed way to expand your family (if you have the funds to do so—that's a whole other rabbit hole). But did you know that just like 1 in 5 pregnancies end in a miscarriage, 1 in 5 adoptions end in disruption? This is often referred to as adoption fall-through. In the world of domestic infant adoption (our chosen route), this can look like a biological mother changing her mind, another biological family member stepping in to parent, or unforeseen complications at birth.

While there are many reasons why adoption fall-through can be a *good* thing for the child or biological family, we as the adoptive parents still face the very real possibility of having our hearts broken after becoming attached to a child, and that's freaking scary.

If your journey to parenthood involves infertility or adoption fall-through, the struggle to feel whole and remain faithful is a very real issue. You look around and see families with as many healthy children as they desire. You see some women conceiving accidentally—*excuse me??* You hear about abortions and feel rage. When our parenting timeline doesn't pan out the way we long for, the entire world can feel like one big rub-it-in-your-face moment.

If you haven't read it on enough coffee mugs, may I remind you that it's okay to not be okay. In fact, the only way to become okay is to let yourself feel the full extent of your grief. This particular notch on the timeline is heavier. It just is. The disappointment, heartache, and anger are valid feelings, but once you acknowledge them, you can use them to inspire beauty in a life you never dreamt. When your dreams are extinguished, new hope emerges. Your capacity for love, your ability to create connection, and your heart to nurture are all very much still intact. You are real and you are whole. Feel it, know it.

FROM THE ASHES

I don't want to write about this. I don't. But I must, because if I refuse to acknowledge the most gut-wrenching and paralyzing left turns in life, then I'm ignoring the humanity—the mortality—on which we all hang our hats. That's the whole thing right? Timelines end at our deaths. And as parents, it's hard to tell the difference between us and them. Me and my baby.

Whether your child is one of the approximately 1,160 children each year who die of pediatric cancer, one of 800 to pass from drowning, one of 3,600 infants to succumb to SIDS, one of 400 lost to SUDC, or was called to heaven for a different reason in childhood, adolescence or adulthood, your life—your entire being—will change its shape. Permanently. There's no getting around that.

Have you heard of Brené Brown's term "foreboding joy"? It's that pit in your stomach when you realize everything is too lovely. *When's the shoe going to drop?* I feel that on a daily basis in the presence of my children. I attempt to manage it so to appreciate the joyful moments and the tremendous gushes of love, but it creeps in incessantly. I know I'm not alone. I know many, if not most, mothers experience at least some level of anxiety over their children's wellbeing even when they're perfectly healthy. It's why the Elizabeth Stone quote rings so true: "Making the decision to have a child—it is momentous. It is to decide forever to have your heart go walking around outside your body."

Losing a child is a depth of trauma that outweighs that of losing a parent because that's not the natural order of things, but I'm going to talk about coping with my mom's death in relation, as it is the grief with which I'm familiar. In the weeks and months following her passing, I did not understand why everyone said I was so strong. My brain reacted a bit like this: *If I don't go to work, I will not have a place to live or food in my mouth. If I ignore my friends, I will never get out of bed. If I don't get out of bed, how will I eat? None of these things make me strong. I'm just surviving because I have no other choice.*

With child loss, parents may look like they've achieved basic survival, but I assure you they haven't. They didn't. They became ashes, and rose a completely new person.

Child rearing is the one part of life that is, in fact, supposed to be linear. For a child to die before the parent is a true break in a timeline. I often think about my grandmother instead of myself when it comes to my mom—hers was the heaviest loss.

In the achiest, most unfair way possible, parents of angels watch other families celebrate birthdays, graduations, and other sequential milestones—their own story cruelly severed.

It may seem trivial to bring up the feeling of inadequacy that accompanies child loss, for the pain and rebirth trumps anything else, but this whole book is about battling the constant nagging voice that tells us we should be at a different place in our lives right now than where we currently are. Child loss, no doubt, interrupts our plan.

Earth-shattering loss doesn't change the truth that your life is not behind—it cannot be. If you are a bereaved parent, your Today is missing a piece. Your worth, your validity, your purpose in being alive is not. You are very much whole in being needed, wanted, and powerful. Your existence, while undeniably altered, lights up its own invaluable path, just as you are and for all you were created to be. God is still here, and so are you.

THE MENTAL LOAD

It's no secret that the push and pull of parental expectations as presented by modern day society are enough to drag any mom beneath the surface. In a world where we "can do it all," we are given no wiggle room or grace to do anything less than everything, which is far more exhausting than it is liberating.

Thanks to technology, you can now pump at work, so there's no excuse not to give your child precious breast milk with all its antibodies and unicorn dust while also bringing home the bacon. You must now provide milk AND bacon because otherwise are you even a strong woman? But also please don't make anyone in the office feel uncomfortable, and please ensure the 15-minute pumping sessions don't take up any minutes. You can bend time, no problem. Remember—you can do it *all*.

Being a strong woman is defined by having a "real" job, by the way, so make sure you're giving your kids an example of a strong mom in the workforce! But don't let anyone else raise your children, otherwise they'll form deep-seated issues related to not spending enough time with their mother. Daycare is just an excuse not to raise your own kids.

You still have to prioritize you-time, like going out with friends and taking baths! Just don't have too much fun because you have responsibilities now. It's time to grow up and settle down.

Kids need discipline, but no time-outs, loss of privileges, or ever using the word "no."

Screen time will make your children depressed by the time they reach elementary school, but if your child makes a peep on the airplane, you are unbelievably inconsiderate. Figure it out.

P.S.- Let your husband touch your boobs, and if you don't feel sexy, you need to loosen up and stop being so wrapped up in your kids. Then when you're done with sexy time, don't forget to go nurse the baby (from those same boobs). She's hungry.

Honestly, that collection of looming guilt-trips and contradictions doesn't even scratch the surface. You want to get into baby sleep? Adolescents on social media? To use or not to use water floaties? Cow's milk? School projects? Extracurriculars? Chores, pacifiers, introducing solids, potty training, The Talk, curfews…the list of controversial subjects with two or more "scientific conclusions" about how they'll affect your children is basically endless. At this point, I wouldn't be surprised if there are two different studies about hairbrushes, one saying if your teenage daughter uses a square hairbrush she'll get better grades in school, and the other saying if she uses a round hairbrush she won't struggle with depression. I mean, *really*.

The problem with parenting opinions is they are presented as facts. *Just look at the research.*

But not that other, contradicting research that doesn't back up my opinion.

It's exhausting to try and figure out which doctor, scientist, or mommy blogger is right. Make the wrong choice and you're basically dooming your child. (So they make you think.)

Oh, and if figuring out how to raise your children without scarring them isn't enough—do it while looking good, why don't you? Sure, pictures of moms owning their stretch marks go viral, but I've yet to meet a single mother who doesn't wish she could fit back in her pre-baby pants. Not a one. All that my-body-is-so-awesome-pooch-and-all is a flight of fancy—a great idea in theory, easiest said confidently in the light of day while remaining a quiet whisper of shame each night as a woman undresses and puts her fat jeans back in the drawer next to the pair she hopes will fit again someday. (If you wash your jeans every night, you're doing it wrong.)

The pressure to get it all right, from your parenting choices to your self-love, is crushing. I want to include here the words I wrote on my blog six months after my first child was born, because I think they really highlight how crushing societal expectations can be on parents—particularly moms:

> Breastfeeding is a word, an act, an expectation that has literally eaten away at me for six months. I can't do it. Not successfully. Not in the way all my friends and family have done it. Not where I power through the pain at the beginning to see light on the other side, when the baby eats happily to his heart's content.

Or the baby dives into his mom's chest for comfort when he's scared or tired or just plain misses her. I'm nursing, but in short, unsatisfying spurts, where my baby tries to humor me for a few precious minutes, popping on and off as I serve up half an ounce that he graciously works so hard to get.

He looks up at me with furrowed brows, politely asking if he can be done pretending to suck because we both know there's nothing coming out.

I learned months ago to stop begging him to keep trying. I get up, make him his six ounces of formula, which he happily downs as I wonder if that was the last time I'll ever feel the sensation of feeding my child. Each time, I'm painfully aware that my supply is almost nonexistent, and that the bonding ritual I treasure so deeply is going to reach an end at any moment.

When I first fed Anders the day he was born, I felt proud. He latched as well as any brand new baby could, and I was mentally prepared to do whatever it took to nurse him for a year or more. Those first 36 hours, I dutifully set my alarm for every three hours, day and night, to feed my angel. Then he was swept away to the observation ward, followed by a brief stay in the NICU due to a manageable infection. I was still an inpatient myself, so even though I wasn't right next to him, I shuffled my way down the long hallway to his room every three hours, making sure my baby boy knew that Mom was here to provide for him no matter what.

But then Aaron and I were sent home, while Anders had to stay in the hospital to receive his antibiotics through an IV. We knew it was coming, so I learned how to use the hospital pump, and spent the whole day pumping after each feeding in order to fill enough miniature bottles to last him through the night without me. It was the night after Christmas, and while my little boy was attached to tubes, laying helplessly in a clear plastic bin, I went home in tears, blankly staring at the empty car seat and telling Aaron that this just wasn't right. It wasn't how it was supposed to be.

We pulled our pump out of the corner of the nursery closet where I'd stowed it with the expectation that I wouldn't use it for the first few months. That night, I set my alarm for every three hours so not to lose my beginner's supply and sat in the glider all alone in Anders' dark, empty nursery, trying to wrap my head around the last 48 hours as I hooked my aching body up to a machine and listened to its harsh rhythmic buzzing.

The next seven nights, we were allowed to stay with him in the hospital, so I went back to nursing as planned. Even though it was awkward because he was attached to a three-foot tube and neither of us knew what we were doing, we did it together. I was proud when the lactation consultants came in and said I was doing a great job, despite fighting off tubes and wires that made changing sides an absolute nightmare.

I was almost two weeks into motherhood, and I'd never been able to carry my baby in my arms more than three feet. From his plastic bin where he slept, into the tiny hospital bed I shared with my husband. That's it.

But I was nursing. And that was something to hold onto as I kissed my sleeping husband's lips at midnight on New Year's Eve after I'd woken up for my scheduled feeding session.

Before we left the hospital, Anders successfully regained his natural post-birth weight loss, leaving the hospital a few ounces heavier than he was when he was born. Nurses and doctors told me how great we'd done with feeding him. He was thriving. His infection was gone. He'd be okay.

We got home, and he didn't sleep for 24 hours. Well...he did four hours total in 24 hours. So I guess he technically slept a little. I did not. I weighed myself and noticed I'd lost 30 pounds in the two weeks since he was born. Probably because the hospital food was gross and I'd prioritized sleep over food. I made a mental note to myself to eat more, because even though I needed to kick the baby weight, I knew that I had to feed myself in order to feed my baby.

His sleep didn't improve. It wasn't the normal newborn sleep issue...it seemed more frantic than that. He was constantly upset. He incessantly turned to my breast, but then would pop off, crying even louder than before.

We went to the hospital five days later for his first checkup, and he'd lost weight. No more "Great job, Mama." No more "Wow, look at all that milk you're making!" Instead, I was told to keep trying, with a gentle look of pity and concern. "Keep feeding every two to three hours, but come back in a week for another weight check."

The first few days following that appointment, I told myself it was a fluke. It was just gas pain, of course, that caused the crying. It had to be. I'd made plenty of milk in the hospital! He'd reached his birth weight, plus some! Milk supply doesn't just disappear. I'd been bringing him to breast whenever he wanted it, feeding him every three hours even if he was sleeping, and doing everything like I'd been taught in my breastfeeding classes. It was a fluke that he lost weight. Just a fluke.

He kept crying. Louder still when I tried to nurse.

Finally I joined him in the crying. I couldn't

stop. Not because of the pain of a little monster grappling with one of the most sensitive parts of the female body, causing blisters and scabs and raw skin. Not because I hadn't slept longer than 45 minutes straight in three weeks. Not because I still couldn't walk normally. But because I knew my baby was hungry. I knew he wasn't thriving. I was starving this beautiful child who I loved more than I knew possible.

I had to stop. Stop ignoring my painful instinct that told me Anders wasn't growing like he should. Stop ignoring the people who love me most, who told me I needed to disregard the blogs and statistics and studies and Facebook statuses and well-meaning friends, and just FEED my baby. Stop crying. Stop analyzing. Stop fearing. Stop agonizing.

In the aisle of Target, looking less like humans and more like swamp creatures, Aaron hastily Googled "best formula," and I grabbed a purple tub from the shelf. I felt shame as I walked past other moms in the aisle, wondering if they thought I was lazy or selfish.

Bless the one woman who looked at Anders in his stroller and asked, "How old?"

"Three weeks," I answered.

"Congratulations for getting out of the house!

You're doing great," she smiled.

We need more people like that woman in the world. She has no idea how much that one little pat on the back meant in that moment.

It's not that I was emphatically anti-formula. Not at all. I just believed the lie that you can always breastfeed if you TRY hard enough. The truths and the opinions run together: Breastfeeding women tend to be more educated. Breast milk has antibodies that formula doesn't. Formula interferes with a baby's sensitive digestive system. Breastfed babies bond better with their mother. Breastfed babies feel safer.

All I knew was that I'm a strong, determined, educated woman. Of course I'd breastfeed. I'd give my baby antibodies and nutrients that only a mother's body can provide. I'd stay up all day and all night if it meant nurturing my child. I'd make lactation cookies and drink mother's milk tea. I'd take nine fenugreek pills a day and have oatmeal every morning. I'd form a speed-dial relationship with a lactation consultant, help my child latch perfectly, and pump after each feeding to increase my supply. I'd stop pumping and only bring my baby to breast to stimulate. I'd chug water all day and sleep at every opportunity to recharge my body for the sole purpose of sacrificing it.

And I did all of those things.

I also self-loathed. I wondered if I misread cues and didn't let him cluster feed enough, resulting in losing my supply. I wondered if not eating in the hospital caused the drop, even though in the hospital is when he gained the most weight on my breast milk. I wondered if I should've told the nurse in the observation ward "no" when she asked if she could give him one ounce of formula because they needed to prepare him faster for his blood work, and I said "okay" because I didn't know what to do as a first time, terrified mother whose two-day old baby needed blood work. I felt embarrassed, guilty, and envious when I watched my friends successfully nurse their thriving babies.

And I still do.

I logically know I did everything possible to exclusively breastfeed. That word: "exclusive." It races through my mind Every. Single. Day. People ask me if I'm breastfeeding and I say, "Yes, plus some formula."

"Oh, so not exclusively," they say.

My heart sinks.

I've nursed him as much as any exclusively breastfeeding mother. I have refused to miss any feedings for fear of losing the 0.5-2 ounces of milk I produce, depending on the time of day.

Aaron has never taken an overnight feeding. He's offered, but I don't want to skip and risk losing milk. I turned down a huge promotion at work and point-blank told my CEO it's because I can't pump instead of breastfeed—I need to be with my baby. (He ultimately allowed me to take Anders to work, so I took the job.)

In the four times I've hired a babysitter since Anders' birth six months ago, I pumped during each and every feeding time, even when it was supremely inconvenient. I remember once not being able to find anywhere to pump in Downtown Williamsburg other than a single stall restroom with a line forming. I hastily plugged my pump into the wall, hoping standing water on the counter wouldn't touch any of the pumping parts, and quickly attached the funnels beneath my shirt. I stood there under the fluorescent lights, staring at the cracking brown wallpaper for about two minutes with nothing coming out, shaking and sweating in my uncomfortably vulnerable state, knowing I was holding up everyone outside the door.

I began to panic and cry.

I shoved everything back inside the bag and retreated back to our little table at the café. I was shaking so badly that my husband had to take the bag from me to properly stow all the parts, including the still-empty bottles. My sweet husband had planned this getaway for my 30th birthday, and the first half of the day was clouded by my mini-panic attack. He was upset with himself for not thinking through where I could pump. I was traumatized and frustrated and guilty.

But even with all of that—even through the effort and dedication and unwavering priority—Anders is not exclusively breastfed. So to many mothers, I don't qualify as a breastfeeding mom.

How defeating.

I know it's not about other people. It's about the fact that I've bent over backwards to give my angel as much breast milk as I possibly can since I know it's good for him. But still. To do all that and still be reminded of not reaching the "exclusivity" rank...it's demoralizing.

I'm reminded of his formula intake at every turn. When people ask how he's sleeping, and I tell them that he takes his naps in his crib and sleeps 10-11 hours most nights, the immediate response I've heard over and over is, "Oh he takes formula, I forgot." Never mind the fact that I spent tireless, backbreaking hours helping my baby learn how to sleep in his crib. Never mind the fact that many of my friends with restless sleepers have said that adding formula to their baby's diet hasn't extended sleep whatsoever.

Even the less outright comments get to me. When someone mentions that her baby nurses for comfort, or that she can't wean her child off of the breast, or talks about the breast milk in the freezer...I feel a distinct pain in my chest. No one means harm by these comments, of course, but they rip me apart.

Logically, I know Anders is fine. He's more than fine. He's amazing! People constantly talk about how happy he is, my doctor tells me how healthy he is, and I know how loved he is. I focus on those things, and if the formula conversation is broached, those are the things I spout on about. I tell people it's no big deal. That at first I fought it, but now I'm grateful for it.

And that's true. But I'm writing this to tell the world that it still stings. No matter how logical I am, no matter how many kind friends and family and strangers tell me it's okay, I still feel like a failure. It has spilled over into my self-confidence, affecting everything from my weight to my inclination to socialize.

Like I said, I'm not anti-formula, nor do I admonish mothers who willingly choose that route. It just wasn't the one I wanted, and I'm not sure when or how I will ever fully feel like I've given Anders everything I could as his mom. I have this weird voice telling me that if I'd given birth to him 100 years ago before formula was invented, he would have died. I am not enough as his mother. Once, he had a full meltdown in the car where he was crying so hard he literally couldn't breathe while we were stuck in traffic. I pulled over to try to calm him, cursing myself because if only I had adequate milk in my breasts, maybe he'd latch and nurse and finally catch his breath.

I'm still scared that he doesn't feel as bonded with me, that he doesn't see me as a source of comfort, or that he will have some sort of health problem down the line.

I think the internet is a beautiful thing. It allows me to connect with my community, and provides us answers we wouldn't otherwise have. But it also creates endless opportunity for comparison and an "expert on everything" society, which can damage people on a very deep and debilitating level. Whether it's motherhood or body image or career status or relationships, we think we have to live up to the "ideal" in EVERY aspect of our lives, even the ones that are very much out of our control.

I'm working on realizing that I can't blame myself for everything, and I'm trying to be "above" caring what others think. But I'm not there quite yet. And I don't want to feel embarrassed for feeling guilty or

> idiotic for caring about opinions, all on top of still feeling how I feel. So I'm owning it in hopes that this helps anyone who might be facing a similar obstacle. To you (and to me): No challenge or failure should determine your self-worth.
>
> I know my self-worth comes from God. It comes from loving others and being kind. It comes from being grateful for what I have and gracious with myself. I'll get over this hurdle eventually, and I hope you do, too.

I did get over that hurdle. I've even breastfed a second baby, watched my oldest son continue to excel, and the worry has dissipated. Funny how time does that. Mom pressure simply doesn't matter in the grand scheme of things, and boy am I grateful I learned that difficult lesson so early on in the game.

ISOLATION

I'm eight months pregnant on my hands and knees, picking up approximately 250 Duplo pieces. I wonder what I look like, then immediately erase the image from my mind because it's too animalistic. Too scary. Like a heavily breathing sea mammal beached on a sandbar. On social media, everyone comments on the cute videos of my toddler cuddling the bump, me baking craving cookies with my husband, and the relaxing Alaska views. But no one knows. No one sees me on my hands and knees every single day at 12:30 p.m. when Anders goes down for his nap. Is this where humility is rooted? Close to the ground, and swiveling my torso the size of Jupiter? It must be.

Young motherhood brings you to your knees.

Cleaning Duplos. Crawling around with your toddler on your back like a baby gorilla. Picking up onion peels strewn on the kitchen floor each night, which entertained the littles so you could cook. Re-shelving books. Providing cheerleading during tummy time. Furnishing human limbs as a living jungle gym. Reassembling wooden puzzles, building plastic animal zoos, and grabbing food scraps from the ground before they make the dog sick. Always alone, always on your knees. In some ways, that's convenient, because whew, child—you need as much prayer as you can get.

I smell. All the time. Why, you ask? Just the sweat. All the sweat. The sweat that begins dripping before I even get to the car, brought on by putting on coats, shoving on shoes that I swear I just bought but *why on earth do they seem so tight*, running back for a snack, dashing the 30-pound infant car seat to the car and getting back inside the garage to grab the toddler before he switches off the heating system to the house. He's now angry because the heat switch is still on, but I must buckle him into his five-point harness while he writhes like an alligator.

Once inside the baby entrapment—I mean car—it's time to recite the entirety of *Pout Pout Fish* until we reach our destination, at which point I do everything I just did but in reverse, then grocery shop like I'm on *Top Chef* because I only have 30 minutes before Baby wakes up and demands to attack my breasts. *Great job, S! You remembered the cheese sticks!* Now time to unload the cart while Toddler tries to grab all convenience items in the check out line. It's like that show *The Floor is Lava* except EVERYTHING IS LAVA.

But wait, there's more!

Now you must do the whole juggle of getting the kids back in the car, but this time with groceries, in a parking lot full of idiots speeding past.

OH THE SWEAT.

The daily grind of survival with little ones is enough to

make any woman feel defeated by the most mundane of tasks. Couple the objective difficulty of doing absolutely anything with the endless contradictions of the Parenting Police, and it's no wonder every mom feels like they're in a black hole all alone. *These other moms are killing it, and God I really need to change my underwear for the third time today because the babies ruined my undercarriage, and OMG I just yelled at my toddler and now he's scarred forever.* Real talk: The third underwear change of the day is a lonely feeling.

Isolation isn't simply a repercussion of hardship, though. It's a result of unparalleled joy, as well. How can you possibly express how it feels when your baby smiles into your eyes? Words and pictures do not capture the weight of your child's head on your chest. The angelic sound of laughter that warps the room into heaven. It's impossible for anyone else to know your children the way you do, from the sly smile to the scar on his leg and how he smacks is luscious little lips. Our love as parents, while relatable as a whole, is custom-made. Each of us experiences it so uniquely, so delicately, so exclusively. It's surprisingly and breathtakingly lonely in its splendor.

The thing is, though, you're not alone. The vast majority of other moms *do* get it. They really do. I don't care if her hair is curled or her child is wearing two of the same socks, I promise that she smells of sweat and goldfish and adoration if you get close enough.

And you should really try to get close enough because the two best ways to manage motherhood isolation is to 1) share your struggles with a fellow mom so that you don't internalize and perpetuate self-blame—plus in sharing you'll often find the humor, and 2) squeeze in some sense of accomplishment that doesn't involve a clean playroom. I won't call this "self-care" because we all know by now that I file that term under "one more thing moms have to do to keep up with expectations," but have a Skype wine date with a friend, read a book, double down and actually complete the baby book, go for a run—anything that will make you say *Man, I'm so glad I did that*. When you know you can still do at least one thing you *want* to do with your free time, the isolation will feel less like jail, and more like the phase that it is.

THE MOMS CLUB

"So excited for you to join the Moms Club!" rang in my ears over and over when I was pregnant with my first baby. I thought it was just a congratulatory platitude, marking my entrance into a relatively common and expected experience. Miraculous—undoubtedly, but generationally customary nonetheless.

Then I gave birth.

No one *really* knows when someone's giving birth. They see pregnant pictures on social media, or viral pregnant dance videos if you're Allison Holker and Twitch. Then BOOM! One day a photo pops up on your feed of the new baby. Were you eating a sandwich while she was pushing it out? Watching *Queer Eye*? (Can you believe??) The life-changing hours in someone else's life are completely insignificant in our own.

Except they're not. Not to this secret, underground, unexpected clan of other moms who become lifelines during the most transformative phenomenon in your lifetime.

In the days leading up to labor, I started getting a few messages on Instagram from women I considered mere acquaintances, along with texts from my real-life friends who were young moms. Everyone who began reaching out had kids under the age of two, freshly aware of what it means to be suddenly thrust into this insane world of motherhood (that I comprehended nearly 0% before entering…because you can't). They asked how I was feeling and genuinely wanted to know the answer. They prepped me with excitement and community and solidarity.

When the day came that liquid suddenly gushed out of my lady area, which—let me tell you—is a *stark* reminder that this whole ordeal is a physical experience *completely* out of your control, I texted a few friends to let them know that labor had begun. I even messaged a few acquaintances-who-care because something told me they should know. *My water broke, Aaron and I are heading to the hospital. Say prayers!*

On the 30-minute drive to the hospital, my good friend called. She'd recently given sudden and accidental birth on her bathroom floor to her first child, so to say she's a superhero is an understatement. I honestly wasn't really open to speaking to anyone in that moment because my contractions had already rendered me mute during each peak, plus my husband is just about the only person on earth who doesn't heighten my stress during tense experiences. But when I saw her name pop up, it felt right. I wanted to hear her voice, and also needed some support from a source of calm and wisdom. (My sweet, sweet husband was a deer-in-headlights just trying not to crash the car. Priorities straight.)

This friend gave me reassurance and confidence as we

approached the hospital. She reminded me of my strength, promised me a positive outcome, and walked me through steady breathing. It was true manifestation of this whole Moms Club thing.

As I labored, I occasionally looked at my phone since the epidural allowed me to function pretty normally minus the ability to walk by myself. (Big epidural fan over here!) Throughout the night—probably because they were up nursing little ones themselves—I received texts and Instagram messages from this unexpected circle that had magically assembled in the days prior. It reminded me of the circle of elephants—how female elephants surround the one in labor to support and protect her.

While the rest of the world would wake up to find a picture of our little boy on Christmas Eve morning, these women wouldn't be surprised. They were there the whole time, giving me encouragement and easing my fears.

Our sweet son arrived seven hours after my water broke, at 4:39 a.m. the day before Christmas, and I began sharing the good news. I'm not one to keep things to myself. Congratulatory texts flooded in. Once things were on social media, "likes" and comments blew up my phone. People seemed genuinely happy for our new addition—this new life entrusted to our very unqualified care.

But let me tell you, it was the Moms Club that became my lifeline. They private messaged me and sent texts that got straight to gritty. *How are you sleeping? Is nursing going alright? Your nipples still intact? I've been praying for your anxiety. I know how scary all of this is. Have you tried witch hazel? Take your laxatives!! If you fold down the diaper at the top, he won't pee through it as easily. I'm sure you're up with him right now at 1 a.m., so just wanted to let you know you're doing great.*

This group of women included a girl I did one pageant with six years earlier. The wife of an old boyfriend's best friend. A college sorority sister I'd barely spoken to in seven years. Mixed in, of course, were my closest friends who'd already had children. All of a sudden they were illuminated, our bond and camaraderie completely unified. They revealed to me their struggles that I never before could've comprehended before I joined their ranks. These women who I considered dear friends became brand new to me. And the ones I barely knew suddenly morphed into fellow warriors on the frontline.

This sisterhood has only expanded in the years since Anders was born. Some of the OG warriors and I don't talk like we did during those first few days of Anders' life, but I'll always think of them as my birth-time angels. When they "like" my photos or I respond to something in their Instagram stories, I know there's an underlying bond. They welcomed me into this new, difficult, wild segment of my life, not because they had to, but because they are part of an ancient tradition of women protecting their own kind.

My close friends with kids are my helpmates, kindred spirits, and confidants. Few words are necessary as we speak the language of moms, completely understanding every experience, passing no judgment, and providing laughter amidst chaos. We exchange advice and articles and frustrations, laying bare the often complex and contradictory feelings that accompany motherhood. They make me feel sane, supported, validated, and fiercely loved. I have non-parent friends who I treasure more than words—no question about that. But when you learn what it feels like to have a child rip out your heart and toddle around the world with it in their hands—that kind of vulnerability can only be understood by another mom. It is debilitating and frightening and beautiful and thrilling. This sisterhood is a straight-up *requirement* for emotional (and physical) survival.

My mom circle expands all the time. We talk about sleep woes, body woes, anxiety woes, cuteness explosions, love bursts, hopes and dreams…all of it.

The Moms Club is real. It's life-giving, life-saving, and a stunning reminder that women are better when we band together. Having children changed my life because the love I feel for those little humans shifted my entire worldview (and schedule), yes. But having children also changed my life because of this extraordinary group of women who fully understand such an intimate part of my soul.

Moms Club, I love you. Those maternity leggings look so cute on you. Let's have some wine and try to get the *Wiggles* theme song out of our heads. Thank you for being my sounding boards, advisors, cheerleaders, and colleagues of life.

INVENTING YOUR OWN BRAND OF PERFECT

According to the 2019 U.S. Census, 1 in 4 children are being raised in a single parent household. The National Center for Learning Disabilities discovered that 1 in 5 children have a brain-based learning disability like dyslexia or ADHD, which requires special attention in order for that child to thrive socially and academically. One in 33 babies are born with a physical defect, which doesn't account for those who develop them as a result of accidents. Around 7% of the U.S. population has a major depressive episode in a given year, including the 80% of new mothers who experience baby blues or postpartum depression. Let me repeat that: 80% of new mothers experience some level of depression.

I'm not going to personally crunch those numbers, but it doesn't take a scientist to figure out that single parents, parents of disabled or sick children, or depressed parents are in every neighborhood, every yoga class, every PTA meeting, every church gathering, and anywhere else where humans raising other humans coexist.

Let's not hide our struggles. Let's view them as possibilities. In this case, your unforeseen parenting challenge is the opportunity for unexpected revelation. Instead of drowning in a timeline that was never promised or even common, rational, or utopian anyway, you can fill the space around you with less constrained ideas of perfection. What does a perfect family unit look like in *your* reality, exactly as it is?

What do you get to learn that will help your children flourish? There's a great big world out there full of subcultures and communities based on potentially unwanted snafus of traditional timelines and parenting encounters, paving the path to friendships that are oh-so-tough to develop once you've graduated from dormitories and collegiate a cappella rehearsals.

You get to feel joy when you watch your child accomplish something infinitely harder for them than for the general population. Their strength is magnified. You can lean into snuggles on the couch on your bad days, and deeply embrace the good days instead of coasting through them. Your faith is refined and sharp and ready.

My mom died before she met her grandbabies. Before she witnessed me as a mom, or even as a wife. I had always assumed that when my children were biting my nipples, throwing blocks at each other, or getting insecure about their leg hair, my mom would be there to guide me through it (not that I knew biting nipples was a thing until it happened). *Mom, how, exactly, do you make it to church every Sunday when service falls right in the middle of naptime?*

Those answers can no longer come from her, and yet I could go on and on about the beautiful parts of my life that all point back to the turning point of my mother's death. Of course I wish she were still here, but I am so darn grateful to be who I am and where I am. Would I have met my husband if she were still alive? Have the kids I do? The friendships proven and the faith forged in fire? I love my life, and to change a piece of it—even a tragic one—would be to sacrifice my greatest joys.

This trade off goes for every aspect of our lives. Parenthood aligns with the Dream for very few. Consistently fighting the good fight against bitterness and disappointment means inventing your own brand of perfection. Doesn't that sound cool? *Invent your own brand of perfect.* It sounds cool, and it'll be the root of your joy, too. Trust me.

THE JOY OF PARENTING

God, babies are so cute. I have Googled "cute aggression" so many times at this point that I'm afraid Child Protective Services is going to ping my address. I could write an entire thesis about the desire to squeeze cheeks. I'm a baby cheek addict. And baby rolls. So doughy! Now I want a sugar cookie! Don't even get me started on gummy smiles. If I could request one thing from God, it would be that babies remain toothless just a little longer.

I know parenting is tough. I know we feel behind and overwhelmed and inadequate. But we've already talked about all of that. Now let's talk about why we find ourselves missing these little nuts once they're asleep, even though we've been anticipating bedtime since the minute they woke up.

A popular "finding" that seems to circulate the web is that parents are less happy than their non-parent counterparts, particularly in the United States. Sometimes non-parents will use this as evidence that their decision to remain childless is, in fact, the better route to a fulfilled life.

Ah, Westerners sure do love a context-free proclamation.

Fun times.

If you truly dissect the research, the things that make parents in the United States less happy are things like a lack of workplace flexibility, leave, and pay—not the kids, themselves. Unhappiness is not inherent to parenthood. It's inherent to parenthood *in the face of unsupportive circumstances*.

You see, parents are unhappy *because* their kids make them so happy. When we fully engage with the unbreakable, pure, and completely saturated love that magnetizes us to our children, we experience the highest level of joy possible. To drown out the noise of confusion and guilt, let go of our shortcomings outlined by online gurus, and just allow ourselves to be fully present with our children—that is to know love. To experience elation. To understand connection.

And all of that joy—well, all of that comes *because* parenthood is hard, not *despite* it being hard.

My mother taught me that the surest, fastest path to joy is to develop strength in uncertain circumstances. This is why she sent me dog sledding with nine strangers after my first life-in-shambles heartbreak. Such a boss mom move.

Parenthood is one, big, exhausting yet extraordinary dog sledding trip. After a huge adventure that knocks you to the ground, then heaves you up into elation, you remember the important things in life. You recognize your worth. You feel powerful and connected to the world around you.

Parenthood is going through that tumultuous and rewarding cycle day in and day out.

Imagine how refined your perspectives become. Imagine how strong you become both physically and mentally. I am convinced that being a mother is the best way to explore the depths of your capabilities.

Aside from what parenthood does to heighten our happiness and refine our souls, it's just plain fun. It's fun to relive your childhood by hunting for slugs and reading books by lantern light. It's fun to throw rocks in the pond instead of mindlessly scrolling through social media. Fun is feeling their sweet, soft cheeks cuddle against you while watching *A Goofy Movie*, all of a sudden sympathizing with Goofy instead of Max. *He just wants to spend time with his kid, man!*

You get to dance in the kitchen, kick soccer balls, attend school plays, and rediscover the magic of Santa and the tooth fairy and homemade popsicles.

Parenthood is hard, but boy is it the absolute best thing on earth. There's no ahead or behind. There's just the glorious, exuberant, precious gift of raw, unrelenting love as it unfolds uniquely and perfectly before you.

CHAPTER 6

friendships

SORRY FOR THAT ONE TIME IN COLLEGE

"Friendship is so weird. You just pick a human you've met and you're like 'yep, I like this one' and you just do stuff with them."
– Bill Murray

In 2015, Taylor Swift brought us The 1989 World Tour and with it, her Squad. All of a sudden everyone was like, *Wait, do I have a squad? Why is Serena Williams not in it? How do I get Gigi Hadid's number?* Overnight, Instagram was saturated with #squadgoals, as if it wasn't already a popularity contest of "likes." Now it actually seemed to matter if your "likes" were grounded in group pictures of your friends in matching one-pieces with "Bae Watch" plastered on the front, or "candids" laughing together in a pumpkin patch.

I am an unapologetic Taylor Swift fan, so don't go thinking I blame Tay for this phenomenon. She was just a 20-something who happened to start a movement she probably didn't even mean to start in the first place. This past year, she blessed us with her 'Lover' album (then 'Folklore' as I was editing this—eek!), and if that isn't reason enough to forgive her for any accidental trendsetting, I don't know what is.

Frindships have been used as a form of hierarchy long before 2015. I just think that's when this blatant assertion of exclusivity through unabashed broadcasting became a viable option for non-celebs. This need to look accepted, privy, and breezy clawed its way out of the high school cafeteria and onto our computer screens, hungrily chomping at the bit for fresh recognition. Friendship became its own pressure-driven entity, seeking quantity and public acknowledgment in the form of tagged wine memes and selfies during Restaurant Week.

Confession: I don't have a Squad.

I have lots of deep, meaningful, lasting friendships spanning 1-25 years, and there are separate pockets within this broad, life-giving circle of mine. No singular, unified Squad.

I have sorority friends and college a cappella friends. (Yes, I lived *Pitch Perfect* and I'm here to tell you that the movie is alarmingly accurate.) Childhood friends and high school chorus friends. I have pageant friends, church friends, mom friends, old coworker friends, and ex-boyfriend friend circle friends. I feel a deep bond and attachment to each individual I call a friend, no matter what bucket they fall into. With some, we FaceTime regularly. Others, we see each other at an annual reunion. Still others, we text out of the blue and that's enough to remain sisters who can rely on each other for absolutely anything.

Sincere friendships are rooted in undocumented shared

experiences. Being woken up at 2:30 a.m. by a call from the police four states away because your friend's purse was stolen and she listed you as the emergency contact. (Purse was found!) It's committing to a rotating dinner each Friday night when you move to a new area, getting to know other families at church until it no longer feels like a chore. Friendship is talking about your sex drives during the second trimester, surprising each other with baby sprinkles, and cleaning out your mom's closet together after she rapidly dies of aggressive cancer. It's crying about a breakup and having happy hour wine dates to fill the empty time. It's forgiving each other after a horrifically embarrassing night in college when you combined heartbreak with alcohol and turned into some sort of werewolf who could only howl and swat anyone trying to help.

Friendships require life: Face-to-face conversations, sharing meals, learning preferences, providing support during painful losses and a hands-on cheering section during victories. We must breathe real breaths around those we are lucky enough to share our lives with, and we must value those hearts as we would our own lives—because what is our life at all if not enriched by the relationships we foster?

Vitalizing friendships can be developed from scratch no matter who you are or what stage of life you're in. And old ones can be repaired, advanced, or reignited. As with any good thing, this process takes time, commitment, and pinot noir. You needn't compare your budding friendships with those of your coworker, who has had the same eight friends since freshman year.

Friendship cannot be about insecurities and regret. Your community will not look like anyone else's. It might be like mine—multifaceted, broad, and individually-driven. It might be a strand of four chords, each of you as tight to the others as you are as a whole. A Squad, if you must. It might start when you are in diapers or it might begin right now, today.

FEMALE FRIENDSHIPS

While we live in a more depressed and disconnected time than ever, we also live in an era where women are consciously choosing to support one another. Cattiness is out and inclusivity is in. What what!

Us ladies are finally tired of the boring narrative that we can't get along. There's this stigma that women cannot communicate with one another rationally, that we hold grudges based on emotional retaliation, and form competitive wedges that inhibit our ability to work alongside one another. Finally—FINALLY!—we are tearing that page out of our story, and making a heavy-handed, loud, and intentional effort to flip the script.

So get on board! I promise you that this roaring steam engine wants you on it. Forget the girls from high school who called you fat. Forget the female boss who tried to suppress your career. Too-da-loo to your overly competitive sister-in-law. I mean, you'll still see her at Christmas, but you get the idea. (On the record, I have the greatest sister-in-laws on the planet.) *All* of us will benefit from banding together because this movement is taking off whether we claim our seat or not. The voices of women supporting other women are getting louder, clearer, and as piercing as when we cackle during girls night. Sorry not sorry.

Unlike the nonexistent relationship train, this sisterhood one is real and all are welcome. The goal is to pack as many people aboard so that the world can't ignore its power. Because when women are on fire together, the force of creativity, self-awareness, love, and intellect cannot be matched. Women are gifted with the extraordinary aptitude for spiritual, fervent rapport, and when cultivated in a unified Care Bear Stare, it can shine a light so bright that we mend souls, stop wars, and influence generations.

I promise you that this level of connection is not far from your reach. It is a follow-up text to the woman who gave you her business card in Safeway. It is a chicken Alfredo bake and six-minute drive to the doorstep of that mom whose husband is deployed. It is a seven-hour bus ride to spend a holiday weekend with a girl you met a few times back in the day and have kept in touch with online. Any one of those ideas might sound daunting or exhausting or awkward, but I promise you that friendship is the key to the kingdom—God certainly made it clear through Jesus' life that it's the key to His.

And I promise with all my might that you are not the only one standing in front of the door, afraid to open it for fear of rejection. Plenty of people are right there with you, just waiting for someone to make the first move.

THE ADULTHOOD DROUGHT

You are a people person. We all are. Even natural hermits like Yours Truly, who viewed mandatory Covid quarantine as a gift from the heavens and prefers being happily nestled in her home away from youths, people who talk on speakerphone in grocery stores, and gatherings that require pants.

It's been highly proven that a sense of belonging drives down depression, amends aggressive behavior, and even contributes to a longer life. You can spew that you don't care what anyone thinks of you all you want, but at the end of the day, you need to feel acknowledged, wanted, and needed.

Too often we're looking for belonging in the wrong place, using the wrong tools with the wrong expectations. If the image chapter didn't underscore the ridiculousness of "like" culture enough, let's revisit that notion here. Notifications of dozens or hundreds or thousands of "likes" are not an indication of belonging (or millions, but that would be assuming a Kardashian is reading this book, in which case, hi, please share how much you like it and tag me on your Instagram, thanks!). If it were that simple, everyone with massive amounts of followers would feel deeply confident and engaged with the world, not desperate and insecure like the vast majority, who occasionally admit to living each day with the empty hope to go viral.

If these popular digital personalities who seem to always be surrounded with other beautiful people don't actually have fulfilling friendships that combat loneliness, then you better start looking elsewhere for examples of meaningful companionship. As in, offline. Big news: The answer does not exist on social media. Yes, it's important to know that other people feel just as isolated as you do in comparison culture, but resolution will not be found in simply sharing the experience of loneliness with others while still remaining fundamentally lonely.

Despite celebrity confessions surrounding loneliness, many of us still wonder why we don't have a friend with a boat who throws fun beach parties or can't fill an entire booth full of trendy fashionistas for brunch. Well, I am happy to stop your wondering with a simple answer: You're probably just older than 23 and/or don't live near your old high school. Read on:

A 2019 study by OnePoll in collaboration with Evite suggests that the average American hasn't made a new friend in the last five years.

Hold up—five years?

Correct.

That feels like a long time to not befriend someone new, but you may also find it refreshingly dismal to know that everyone else is no better at making friends than you are.

Fifty percent of friendships are forged in high school and

31% in college. Basically, once you're an adult, it's extremely normal to have trouble establishing new friendships that actually take place outside of the office. Netflix is your new BFF, replacing hobbies that expose you to new people (more on that in Chapter 7), and according to the 2016 U.S. Census Bureau, 1 in 4 people live in a different city or area from where they grew up. Meaning it's not all Netflix's fault.

High school friends fade as proximity gets the best of friendships beyond the occasional prompted birthday wish on social media. There go 50% of our likely-to-be long-term friends! College friends are even less likely to live in the same location after graduation, as most return to their separate hometowns or take jobs all across the country. Another 31% of our potential lifers bite the dust.

The magical trio of friendship—availability, proximity, and shared interests—is hard to align when classrooms don't pile you on top of your peers. You must find solace in the normalcy of the adult friendship drought, but also the gumption to put in a little work so that you can quench your biological needs of socialization and belonging.

Forming friendships requires bravery. For some reason, most of us expect friends to fall into our laps, similar to the wishful thinking that our soulmate will magically step through the TV screen without us ever having to leave our cozy couch.

Think of making friends like dating. Unless you're like my husband and me who basically fell in love in one week, dating someone tends to get more comfortable over time. Same goes for friendships.

When I moved back to my hometown at age 27, I didn't have many friends in the area. Most of my high school friends had long since moved away, and none of my college friends were from the same place I was. The only people I knew were a circle of friends I'd met through my ex-boyfriend (St. Nick!) right after college, who I'd kept in touch with here and there over the years. As much as it felt a bit odd to build a network using contacts from my now-married ex, I figured I had to start somewhere if I was going to avoid getting tipsy on my parents' expensive wine every Saturday night and habitually passing out in their guest room. Don't get me wrong, there are few activities I enjoy more than having too much wine with my family while singing show tunes at 10 p.m., but a healthy 27-year-old can't rely on such festivities as her only social outlet.

Or can she? Maybe I've gone about this all wrong.

Anyway, I leaned into the ex-boyfriend friend circle. Is it weird that he and his wife ended up being invited to my wedding? Don't answer that.

Upon my move back to Virginia Beach, one of his friends invited me to a weekly girls night to watch *Revenge*, drink wine, and talk about cute dogs, relationships, and hot coworkers. I'd met the other women before, but certainly wasn't close to them. Honestly, they intimidated me like no other when we first met years prior, back when I was with my ex. In all fairness, I was 23 and he was 36, so they likely thought I was a poor, sad little thing. Which I definitely was.

The first few girls nights were enjoyable, but I was nervous. Staying home felt like the less tiring option. Natural introverts like me can feel winded after a few hours with people they don't know very well. Nonetheless, I forced myself to go each week because I liked them, and I knew that eventually I'd stop feeling like I needed to be "on." Also because *Revenge* is one of the best TV shows of the decade. Fight me.

Within a month or two, I was helping myself to as much lasagna as I wanted without worrying what they thought, showed up in pajama pants, and genuinely couldn't wait to catch up each week. They became my people, and I still love them dearly.

Friendships require pushing through the initial small talk with a willingness to dive in. Stop waiting for another person to instigate. Stop being offended if someone doesn't invite you somewhere. Stop thinking someone doesn't care if they haven't called in awhile. Stop assuming you aren't meant to be friends because the first few hangouts feel a bit tiring. All of those are just hurdles that your own insecurities, laziness, and defense mechanisms use to keep you from actually taking your happiness into your own hands. We're wired to choose anger and self-pity over effort because it's too intimidating, awkward, or time-consuming to lay a new foundation. You *can* do this!

I'm a huge proponent of casually inviting myself places (no shame), creating my own social opportunities, and calling friends out of the blue. I mean *way* out of the blue—like we haven't talked in two years but one day I get the urge to chat so I pick up the phone on the 15 minute drive to daycare. There's this stigma of looking desperate or "too little too late," but in reality, you're just being a no-drama, low maintenance friend. The best kind.

FRIENDSHIPS ARE YOUR LEGACY

Not long ago, I grabbed the mail from our mailbox, and in it was a pink card with the name of my mom's friend I haven't seen since I was a child. Inside was a gift card for a baby store and a note saying that if I ever needed a mom's advice, she was there for me.

Immediate waterworks.

That morning, I'd been missing my mom even more than usual. *What do I do about the fact that Anders keeps trying to slap his brand new baby sister?? Mom, haaalp!* Then came the card.

My mother remains an active part of my life and her grandchildren's lives through her friendships. Obviously she lives on through family, too, but there's something so unique about the women my mom *chose* to love in life, not by blood, but through intentional alliance. And those women have continued to choose loving *her* by loving *me*, their friend's daughter, whether or not I've seen or spoken to them in five or 25 years.

The truth is, friends see the best in us, not because they're required to through familial expectation, but because they can't help it. That's why they stick with us. Love from friends is a unique kind of unconditional support, and worth every second of investment. My mom knew this. Her friendships were cemented for a lifetime through a faith in God, glorious memories, and proven loyalty. And they stuck with her even past her lifetime.

As we get older and dig deeper into our family lives, raising little ones who take all of our love and energy, leaning on our spouses as primary pillars, and pushing through the daily grind or pursuing personal goals, it can be so easy to let friendships fall through the cracks. I'm not saying that you have to add more to your plate by spreading yourself too thin with social engagements—I know my mom didn't see her friends as often as she did before kids, and that's normal. But when you do have the time, the energy, and the ability to talk to your friends, build memories, have meaningful conversations, or even exchange quick catch-up texts, do it.

Do it for yourself, do it for them, but also do it for your kids. Invest in your friendships, because someday, those friends might be your biggest legacy and support system for your children. They will be the ones who send your grandchildren presents because you can't. They'll write cards that bring your daughter to tears when she doesn't have your phone calls. They'll read her first book and beam with pride on your behalf.

The gift of friendship expands beyond just your own life. It shines into the lives of those you love, too.

YES NEW FRIENDS

When I moved to Alaska in 2019, I was five months pregnant and Mom to a wild 19-month-old boy. My husband and I only knew one person in Ketchikan—a young Coast Guard junior officer who'd been Aaron's right-hand man at a previous station. As much as I adore 25-year-old Uncle Ky Ky, he's not exactly girls night material.

Before leaving my hometown, where my family resided along with the friendships I'd amassed since moving back and marrying Aaron, everyone seemed fixated on how in the world I would survive 3,500 miles away from any semblance of a support system. Not to mention 650 miles away from the nearest full-scale hospital or Target, and in an area of the world where it rains an average of 250 days per year. Oh, and it's dark by 3 p.m. in the winter. Did I mention there's a huge population of bald eagles that could easily snack on our four-pound ~~daugh~~dogter?

Rightfully so, concern was generally Reaction #1.

Except my own.

I cannot tell you the yearning for adventure that filled my soul when I learned we'd been ordered to Ketchikan, Alaska.

Sure, I'd miss my family, friends, and the beachy lifestyle I know best (born in San Diego, raised in Virginia Beach), but who gets to say they've lived in Alaska?? *Rain-shmain—have you seen the mountains? Cold-shmold—my son gets to play in the snow!* And as far as I knew, Ketchikan was, indeed, home to other human beings. Where people live, there are new friendships to be made.

I don't simply toss aside oldies just because I move—in fact, I have a weird amount of close friends all across the country due to how much I've relocated—but "no new friends" is such a lame slogan. Why do the youngins say it these days, even in jest? I want to karate chop this phrase.

You can definitely sit with us. Whoever I'm with.

Even jokingly, "no new friends" hints at being too lazy, close-minded, or intimidated to expand one's social horizons, which in turn expands one's entire worldview. Making new friends for the sake of popularity in numbers is unsustainable and fruitless, however keeping our hearts open toward new people is an absolutely critical element of self-development and hope. New connections remind us that this world isn't stale, and neither are the people in it.

Back to Alaska. Instead of feeling intimidated by the geographical isolation, I was invigorated. Over and over in my head, I thought about how I'd go about meeting fellow moms, how I would befriend them, and how wild it would be in three years to imagine having never met them. I knew that if I put even a little bit of thought into finding them, effort into forming them, and love into maintaining them, I'd be just as at-home in Alaska as I was in Virginia Beach.

And that's exactly what I did—with gusto. Because I had exactly four months before I would need to call someone when I went into labor to watch my not-so-gentle 2-year-old. The clock was ticking to build at least one friendship that could withstand a middle-of-the-night phone call and trust them with my child. No pressure.

Like a mad scientist, I got right to work on my master plan as soon as we arrived. This was my personal roadmap:

Step one: Go to church. Fellowship is a vital piece of our spiritual wellbeing, but even from a secular vantage point—if you want to make friends, go to church. Join a community group. Get in your car and show up every week. My Alaska family group moms have now seen me nursing with no cover, no makeup, and chocolate stuck to the corner of my lips. Things get *real* real when you see the same people every Friday night and there's no official dress code.

Step two: Attend toddler time at the library, rec center, or anywhere else I heard about little people gathering, like the gymnastics place down the street. Strike up conversations with moms until I find one who seems relatable, then charm her on a weekly basis until it's not weird to friend her on Facebook. I found two other friends this way.

Step three: Say "yes" to invitations. This includes that time a woman approached me at Safeway and said, "Sorry if this is weird, but I noticed you have a toddler and are pregnant, and

I'm starting a Bible story time for kids on Tuesday mornings. I'm also a newborn photographer. Here's my card. Text me if you want to join!" Since she started with "Sorry if this is weird" and gave me her number so the ball was in my court, I decided she wasn't a psychopath or serial killer, so I showed up on Tuesday morning. She became a great friend who delivers killer chicken noodle soup when I'm sick, and also took the most beautiful newborn portraits of our daughter three months later. Oh, and she took the cover photo for this book!

At her Tuesday morning story time, I met two other Coast Guard wives who hadn't slept in six months thanks to tiny children, and they, too, became my people. To woo one of them, I secretly found her address and delivered chicken Alfredo to her doorstep (I reference chicken Alfredo a lot because it is universally appealing and my best casserole-type dish offering) when her husband was out to sea, knowing full-well she'd be forced to be my friend if I brought her cheesy pasta. Muahaha. Four months after our arrival in Ketchikan, she threw me the perfect baby sprinkle with eight people in attendance.

Boom. I had formed my circle.

Turns out, Aaron's 25-year-old former shipmate was still the best choice to watch our toddler when I went into labor, because A) a single guy in a remote town in Alaska doesn't really have much else better to do than hang with a 2-year-old for 48 hours, and B) Anders is high-key obsessed with Ky Ky. BUT, any of my new friends would've bent over backwards to be there for me or come to Anders' aid if Ky Ky had a question. (Lucky for him, I'd written an 11-page manual.)

Instead of wasting time wishing your life looked as full as Taylor Swift's special guest list on her 1989 World Tour, focus on giving your heart (and food!) to whoever is in your path, and the value of your friendships will grow twice as fast as the meaningless number of butts in your booth at brunch. When moving to Alaska, my goal was to find just one friend I could call during labor. Instead, I found eight. When you shift your focus from popularity to authentic connection, the world will always deliver.

IT'S NOT ABOUT YOU

Spouses are great. Parents are wonderful. Kids are magic. But they cannot be your everything. Those people hold powerful, necessary roles in your life, but friendship is a different, equally necessary entity. Friends in the flesh give meaning to your life through a web of diverse human beings that ultimately anchor you to society, providing belonging, perspective, humor, motivation, love, and memories to serve your soul.

Without friends with whom you can share your life, you miss out on vital opportunities to experience the wide range of emotion and experiences that fulfill the human need to get outside of our narcissistic inclinations and instead invest in a world much bigger than our immediate surroundings. When we learn about people outside of our families, and witness firsthand a variety of needs, struggles, desires, hopes, talents, histories, personalities, and preferences, we not only get to enjoy the camaraderie, but are also given relief from the exhausting hamster wheel of a self-absorbed lifestyle.

When are you the happiest? Not when you're thinking about how to succeed, patting your back for succeeding, or lamenting how you didn't succeed. Not when you're staring at yourself in the mirror, droning on about yourself to others, or worrying about your own needs. Not even in moments of being proud of yourself and your life. Seriously—fight the "me" culture. It doesn't work for joy.

No—the moments we feel the most content are when we give our energy to other people from a place of love. It's an interesting cycle—how the more we serve others the more we serve our deeper selves. But this cycle is no mystery. It's been proven over and over that pouring into our friendships has the same chemical reaction as volunteerism or being needed—we get a rush of endorphins when our energy is focused on improving someone else's life instead obsessing over our own, leading to a longer, healthier life. Science!

Sitting around a dinner table with friends rarely leaves room for a me-only spotlight. Instead, you share stories, equally listening and contributing, giving your heart and mind room to breathe as they are released from the idiosyncratic, claustrophobic bubble that is our daily inner existence. Doesn't that sound nice?

CHAPTER 7

hobbies & service

FREE TIME

Remember when you were a kid, and you participated in extracurricular activities? Could've been baseball, community theatre, ballet, horseback riding, step team, student council, or maybe just an unstructured hour of hacky sack in the courtyard after school. Those guys intrigued me. Generally speaking, it's hard to be a kid without a hobby.

As we grow up and realize that collegiate or professional athleticism and hobbies aren't in the cards for us (it still stings that I didn't make the 2012 Olympic equestrian team), extracurricular involvement dwindles. Socializing or "me-time" becomes the go-to hobby for young adults in the form of happy hours, brunch, and *Schitt's Creek* marathons.

Somewhere around our quarter-life, we start realizing that maybe we should do something a tad more interesting with our free time. Perhaps join a CrossFit gym or a running club. Learn how to brew beer or cook from-scratch meals. Maybe revisit that old guitar and book a few gigs, or start painting on the weekends. Hobbies slowly build themselves back into our lives, but fizzle out once again as spouses and kids and careers take off. Better luck next time!

"What do you do for fun?" has become an ironic question. *I watch* Stranger Things *and order Chipotle, Barb. That's what I do for fun.* Is the hobby category still a thing on dating profiles? I've been out of the game a long time, but that one always felt like a strain back in my day. *I love to surf! I love to hike! I love to knit!* Yeesh. Does petting my dog count?

This expectation that we "do something we love" outside of work couples with another ideal for how to spend our free time as adults: Activism. Now that political movements and intricate details about every possible threat to humanity and celebrity PSAs saturate our news feeds, we feel more responsible than ever to be a hero. Or at least somewhat vocal about a few chosen issues.

I'm all about problem-solving and tangible action. Yes! Break out of that stifling and trifling Me bubble! The trouble is that we went from skimming the surface to full on drowning in information. Where do we even begin??

I, for one, tend to freeze up when I am hit with the nightly news round up. It's all too much. Velveeta mac and cheese, climate change, the lonely kid in class, contaminated tap water, lipstick, carnival rides, Big Pharma, touch screens in cars, peaceful protesting, social media, inaccurate memes—they can all kill you. If I'm being honest, sometimes I just close my phone and go to sleep because it's all too much. So I'd rather do nothing.

How in the world do I choose which problem to advocate

for or against? Do advocates even make any real change? Is change possible, or is it all too far-gone?

K, time for bed.

I recently heard the phrase "analysis paralysis." It me! [Insert girl-raising-hand emoji.] The more I analyze our world, the more paralyzed I become.

For many, activism is yet one more way to peacock one's awesomeness. Especially for white people. It's a complex, aptly named disorder called the "savior complex"—when we approach good works from the motivational state of proving ourselves to be "good." Gross. No wonder we feel tired. If you're feeling overwhelmed at the thought of helping a cause, maybe you don't actually care all that much about the cause. Maybe you care about looking like you care.

We know we should *love* writing letters to our senators or marching for justice or serving soup, but if you wouldn't go without your phone (i.e. camera), I urge you to reexamine your motives before making your trendy sign or donning a hairnet. And don't just reexamine them—put in the work to refine them. Because the world *does* need you. It really does. For more than just a photo op.

WHAT REVS YOUR ENGINE

Living life in a way that makes you feel truly alive is a recipe only you can develop for yourself. No matter how strongly your neighbor feels about weaving plastic bags into area rugs, you cannot copy her exact ingredients for dexterity or environmentalism.

Case in point: My DMs are full of messages from people raving about my baby books, scrapbooking, and picture-organizing mechanisms that I like to share. The comments often express regret for not making similar compilations, themselves. Whoa there, guys—I just happen to LOVE this sort of thing! I used to spend hours in 7th grade decorating my binders with photos I printed at CVS off of the disposable camera I took to summer camp. Incorporating pictures and glue sticks and bubble words into my life is not hard because it's something I naturally love to do. Of course I still have to force myself to *just do it* on nights I don't feel like breaking out the materials, but it's *my* hobby. It doesn't have to be yours.

You may not know yet what revs your engine, but we all know what's *not* in the recipe: television consumption, interpersonal comparison, and any addiction that inhibits your clarity and functionality (alcohol, drugs, overeating, sexual obsession, etc.). I would even go so far as to say that participation in activities that encompass our minds in a virtual world rather than the tangible one are also not a great idea, unless we're using them as a way to expand our creativity or intelligence. My brother knows I can't possibly write a book without referencing my deep, possibly dramatic disdain for video games, so here it comes! Unless you're inventing new code or analyzing video games for some cool social science experiment, they're a brain-suck, not a hobby. Ugh—there's nothing less attractive than a man breaking a sweat over some fake gun shoot out.

Now that you know what isn't in the recipe for free time full of personal growth, interest, and advocacy, the rest is 100% unique to your tastes. Remember, we're all cookin' up something different here.

What do you enjoy? Even if it's been a while…a year, a decade…since you've done it—spend a few minutes identifying one or a few activities you love (or used to love). Don't judge yourself. Your spirit and body know better than you do.

Listen and do.

By the way, we're not just talking about adult league soccer here. Though I recently found out that Abby Wambach plays on an adult soccer league, so post-college recreation teams suddenly went from awkward dad bods running around in my mind to the straight up Olympics. Adult leagues are legit, you guys! Who knew?

Obvious hobbies like soccer aren't the only pursuits worth your time, to be clear. Do you wish more parents would limit screen time? Then start a Saturday morning "toddlers in the park" club. Reach out to a free book program for kids and ask how you can help. Volunteer to recruit for a Boys and Girls Club. Do something that addresses a tactical way to get kids off their screens, and now you have both a hobby *and* a cause. Boop!

STEALING SOULS

I find myself back on the subject of Taylor Swift and I am not sorry. Have you watched her documentary on Netflix? You should. In it, you'll witness her morph from a country music teenybopper into the world's biggest pop star, then again into a feisty political activist. I mean, she's not running for president or anything beyond her level of expertise (looking at you, Kanye), but she sure knows what she's fighting for on a systemic level.

Something tells me that Tay Tay is a busy woman, yet she has continually transformed herself, both through what she loves (music) and about who she is (her purpose). That was not by accident, nor has it been without tremendous criticism. From my observation, she is an excellent example of taking control of her own time, her own life, her own narrative. (Was "narrative" even a word before she used it in her Kanye statement?)

I just don't see Taylor wasting a whole lot of time on mindless activities when she could be writing a new album or lacing up her social justice boots or planning her takeover of the world. Galaxy? Universe. I mean, hi, she wrote an entire album in Covid quarantine when the rest of us were eating our weight in banana bread.

Neil Postman's book *Amusing Ourselves to Death* is as profoundly relevant today as when he wrote it in 1985. What started as media consumption in the form of television (that you couldn't even pause or rewind!), has now exploded into bingeable content, *Candy Crush*, and video games that somehow look more like real life than real life. Yet caught in all its lifelike HD, we aren't actually living. We are personally and communally sacrificing our existence, rights, and legacies by letting our time absorb into an abyss of mere amusement created by corporations that value their own existence over that of its consumer.

Oof.

Before I go down a Matrix rabbit hole and become engulfed by my feelings about the broad scheme for a powerful few to control the masses without their knowledge, let's switch gears into a basic claim by many scholars: Hobbies are a thing of the past. Not because of some larger government conspiracy or corporation takeover to numb our minds, but simply because we are addicted to screens. (Fine line..?) Simply put, we are quite literally amusing ourselves to death.

We can't pull ourselves away from mind-numbing entertainment—much of which isn't even all that entertaining (unless it's *Tiger King*)—even when we're aware that it's unhealthy. We know it's killing our brains, bodies, and dreams, but walk right on off the plank.

I consider myself a pretty self-motivated person. I set goals and make them happen. I write the words, read the books, wash the dishes, fold the clothes, and sort the toys. But gosh darn it if in the middle of a task, I find myself in a 30-minute scroll hole on Instagram all because I picked up my phone to check the time. The same trap ensnares our availability for hobbies. One second you're Googling cross stitch patterns for your new favorite pastime, and the next, you're watching Trey Kennedy imitate girls during pumpkin spice season.

If you're hitting a quarter-life crisis because you just realized that streaming services have stolen your soul, the first thing you must do is realize that you're not a failure, idiotic, or one of those floating blob people with no purpose in *WALL-E*. And you're certainly not alone, so there's no need to be embarrassed.

As my favorite pastor, author, and personal mentor Randy Singer once said in a sermon: "If your glasses fog up, there's still time." You're breathing. You're alive. You've got an undetermined expanse of time in front of you to change the game.

FUN TAKES PRACTICE

Hobbies, by definition, are not your career—so stop worrying if you're talented enough or worthy of having one. Everybody gets a hobby! You get a hobby and you get a hobby and you in the back! Yes, you! You get a hobby!

Gosh I miss Oprah at 4 p.m. EST every day after school.

Pressure and hobbies do not go together. Nerp. Calm down! Still, whether the goal is to maintain a hobby for life or to develop it into a career, the activities you truly enjoy require you to purposefully choose to *do* them. The question isn't "What do you think about doing for fun?" No, what do you *do* for fun?

Fun. What a funny word. Are adults supposed to have that? Ah, this reminds me of one of my favorite memes, which says "Not a single person asked me how fast I could run in my new shoes today. Being an adult is stupid."

Fun is built into childhood. When does it stop? Why?? Heck, we don't even know what feels fun anymore. I was told parties were supposedly fun, but it wasn't until I was out of college that I realized parties were the least fun. Like, the actual worst.

Turns out no one else can tell you what is fun.

Part of the problem is that we're no longer expected to show up to practice by our coaches, and our mom isn't around to force us to go to rehearsal on weeks we don't feel like it. Fun hobbies aren't always fun. Nothing is *always* fun. Except watching Hamilton on Disney+ over and over and over and over. Don't even try and stop me.

This is why hobbies need to become habits.

Often times, fun gets pushed to the side by responsibilities. We love to write, sing, dance, bake, water ski, do puzzles, practice jumps on our pogo stick...but we need to catch up on work and drive the kids to ballet class. We can squeeze in some fun maybe once a month. A year. A decade. Yikes—how quickly our hobbies can turn into nothing more than nice thoughts if we don't make them habits.

Hobbies provide for us the chance to improve upon something, exert our energy in a healthy manner, bend our creative muscles, and focus on our talents. The sense of joy those byproducts generate is far more complex and profound than the static loop of often shallow and repetitive social engagements, or mind-numbing screen consumption. But the benefits are only lasting if we stick with it.

Don't lie to yourself and believe that if a hobby is worth having, you'll absolutely look forward to doing it every single day. (Or week.) Listen, I want you to choose something that resonates with your soul, but remember—nothing is fun all the time. Hence why you have to make it a habit, or else on inopportune days, you'll decide to stay on the couch or overexert yourself at work instead. Hobbies are hobbies because yes, we enjoy partaking in the activity of choice, but they also require a certain level of discipline that eventually becomes habitual.

My husband loves to cook. The man spends hours each night looking up how to make sourdough starters, the best gadgets and recipes for homemade pasta, new spins on corned beef hash, and the superior meats to cook in an at-home sous vide. He's so obsessed with the kitchen that I often feel like an imposter, doomed for judgment because I do not know the most efficient way to dice an onion, or did not warm the stainless steel pan for the appropriate amount of time before adding olive oil. The kitchen is a dangerous place for our marriage. (But also one of the best.)

Interestingly, for the first three years of marriage, Aaron and I ate Chipotle and store-bought cookies most nights of the week. On the other nights, we ate take-out pho or pizza. Was he busy with work? Yes. Was our kitchen tiny? Yes. Were Chipotle, pho, and pizza delicious? Obviously yes. But it wasn't those excuses that truly kept us from cooking—it was the habit of never turning on the stove.

When we moved to Alaska, we quickly learned that unless we wanted to eat Burger Queen (yes) every single night, we'd have to seriously step up our kitchen game. My son also reached an age where popping open a jar of purée was no longer appropriate. He needed real food, which felt real pesky if I'm being honest. So needy!

Painstakingly at first, I whipped up a roux for all kinds of cream-based sauces that served my second pregnancy *very* well, became a casserole queen, and even encouraged Aaron to lean into his culinary dreams. You might think this took months of a slow build, but it didn't. It was like a light switch. One day, Aaron and I simply began to cook, and we haven't stopped since. Now, our house is overflowing with homemade waffle sliders, sausage gravy of the Gods, Tuscan-inspired spaghetti squash, zucchini latticed lasagna, chicken enchiladas, home-fried apple cider donuts, fresh fries that start with an actual potato, barbecue chicken wings, cauliflower mash with lemon zest shrimp, and—of course—every type of cheesy noodle imaginable.

Our pocketbooks (are those still a thing?) thank us and so do our taste buds. My 20-month-old learned to identify onions and garlic before he could say his own name correctly. He also knew "chai" and "brewskie" first, but that's neither here nor there. Big picture: Cooking in our home became a hobby by way of habit, my friends.

Finding the time to do something is as simple as doing it. My mom loved to say, "Don't try, just do!" It's not about some magical shift in your schedule, the perfect opportunity, or the most convenient stage in your personal life. I would have never written this book if I'd tried to "find the time." Once I realized that the convenient time would never "arrive," I picked up the pen (well, computer) when I was eight months pregnant and raising a toddler. I wrote straight until Jo's birth, and began again five weeks after.

Some might say this was not the wisest time to write my

first book, but you know what? I didn't write a book when I was sans-kids, working only part-time, and sleeping until 9:30 a.m. every morning. So clearly time was just an excuse. As it almost always is.

A habitual hobby will pump massive amounts of joy into your life, and right now is *always* a good time for joy. Especially on newborn sleep and through the endless grind of raising a toddler. I have zero regrets writing my book during this exhausting season of life because by making time in my already insane schedule, I found mental and emotional relief in consistency and creativity.

If you want to be as cool as Abby Wambach, join a soccer league that plays every Saturday morning at 11. Not into organized sports? Set up an easel in your garage and paint every Tuesday and Thursday night for an hour after the kids go to bed. Run every morning. Audition for two musicals at your community theatre each year. Sign up for horseback riding lessons, explore different hiking trails, or commit to knitting 10 hats per month for your local NICU. Give structure—actual expectations and time commitments—to your hobbies so that what you love will become a habit, feeding your happiness, satisfaction, and purpose along the way.

HOBBIES ARE NOT A LUXURY

In 2010, a study headed by Jean Twenge at San Diego State University pointed to a dramatic increase in anxiety and depression in young people since the 1950s. I think this comes as shocking news to exactly no one.

This means that even during the Great Depression, the World Wars, and the Cold War, children, adolescents, and young adults were less depressed and anxious than they are in today's world. Psychological imbalances may not be related to what's going on in the world as much as they're influenced by how people *interpret* the world, alongside their learned and chosen coping mechanisms. (Hint: Screens aren't helping.)

Most importantly, those who feel in control of their wellbeing and personal progress are less likely to be depressed and anxious than those who believe they are victims of their circumstances. We know this from Julian Rotter's Internal-External Locus of Control scale, developed in the 1950s.

During leisure activities, we learn to overcome obstacles, get creative, and relax our brains enough to recharge and prepare for success in other areas of our lives. We develop a stronger internal locus of control.

I think all of us have noticed the drastic shift in school policy, particularly in elementary school, that emphasizes scholastic achievement far more heavily than any form of free play. *Time Magazine* reported: "The American Academy of Pediatrics committee…expect[ed] to discover that recess is important as a physical outlet for children. What they found, however, was that playtime's benefits extend beyond the physical. 'We came to the realization that it really affects social, emotional and cognitive development in a much deeper way than we'd expected,' [Dr. Robert Murray] says."

Our children are being robbed of their ability to develop an internal locus of control because many school systems do not acknowledge the emotional and cognitive benefits of unstructured play. Scores on tests seem to outweigh personal resilience and creativity in educational settings (where most children spend the vast majority of their days, like adults in the workplace), and we wonder why our children struggle to cope in adolescence! They take the easy route of blaming external forces for their misfortune because they're never given the opportunities to learn that they can develop fortitude through creativity, consistency, and resilience.

One of my hobbies since moving to Alaska is hiking, and there's no doubt that getting outside regularly to stretch my legs and complete a melodramatic scan of the trail for bears has improved my ability to focus. When I'm hiking, my mind also drums up some of my most creative ideas that I apply to my writing. When I wave to fellow outdoorsmen (apparently I consider myself an outdoorsman), I am reminded of my belief that most people are inherently good. When I see extraordinary views, my faith reignites.

You see, hiking isn't just about the hike.

Recess isn't just about the monkey bars.

Hobbies aren't just about the hobby.

The benefits seep into every aspect of life, from our strength to our problem solving to our anxiety levels. We're sharpening our core beliefs about ourselves and about the world at large. The world is not out to get you when you're practicing 3-pointers, sewing a scarf, or watering your tomatoes. Your heart is full, your mind and body are engaged, and you are truly present.

SERVICE SHARPENS EMPATHY

When I was in 6th grade, I watched a documentary about India and I was hooked. I wanted to go. Don't ask me why—it truly wasn't a savior complex or a love of brightly colored saris. It was probably the naan. I still live for the naan.

For whatever reason, I found India's culture wildly intriguing. Thankfully, I was raised by a mother who was the queen of "make it happen," so years later when I still couldn't shake this fascination, Mom encouraged me to talk to the pastor of our church in search of an opportunity to make my dream of visiting India become reality. Looking back, I have no idea how my mother always put her rightful fears aside to encourage my dreams, but I'm incredibly grateful she did. I'll try to remember that when my own kids ask if they can fly halfway across the world at age 15.

As it turned out, our church had recently partnered with a church in Chennai, India. It's like God is always ahead of me or something! Crazy how that works! I patted myself on the back for having saved every penny of birthday money ever gifted to me, and signed up for a two-week trip to India with about 20 other people.

A year later, I landed in Chennai (formerly Madras) without a single fear or hesitation—you know, the standard operating level of any 16-year-old from a stable home with a proclivity for musical theatre. As I made my way through the outdated airport and tried to smile kindly at the many, many men asking to take my bag to the taxis for me (some of them grabbing it without my permission), my mind was somewhere between *This feels like a strange amusement park* and *Is this what celebrities feel like?*

I'm not proud to admit this, but at that point in my life, it was all too easy to view people who spoke a different language from me and had wildly different realities as unable to grasp the same concepts I grasped and feel the things I felt. As I clambered into the rickshaw (a three wheel "taxi" with no doors that barely seats two people), I wasn't really in tune with the crowded bustle whirling around me. Some might call it shell-shocked. Others might call it naïve and privileged. I would call it both.

While part of me had definitely geared up to "help" the people I would come in contact with, I had not deeply considered their humanity. Of course my church had prepped us on how "hard" their lives were, but no one really peeled back the layers. These people weren't just impoverished people with no shoes—they were just as smart as I was (many smarter, as seen by their bilingual competence while I loudly said "Hello!"). They developed crushes on their peers and had inside jokes with their friends and felt frustrated having to beg. The emotions I felt? They felt them, too.

It's embarrassing to admit, but I hadn't learned that lesson yet as my rickshaw swerved through traffic. (The driver told us that road signs and lanes were "optional." It's best my mother didn't know this part.)

After our group settled into our bed & breakfast-type accommodations, we set out on our first assignment: Visiting an orphanage full of children whose parents had died of AIDS. Some of the children were sick, others were not, but even the healthy children were cast out from society due to the stigma. Between the ages of 1 and 10 (my guesstimate), each little face lit up when we walked in.

That day was beautiful. We danced, colored, sang songs, and gave them attention their hearts desperately desired. But I didn't feel like a saint. Not at all. It didn't take long for me to realize they were the happiest kids I'd ever met. Way happier than the whiney kids in my neighborhood back home. They loved my hugs, but did not need me to make their lives better. That was clear. In fact, the kids I babysat back in the U.S. seemed to need me to make them happy more than these orphans in India.

I connected with one little girl in particular, a 5-year-old named Lakshmi, with a pixie haircut and knees that were significantly wider than her thighs when she sat cross-legged in my lap. We communicated with custom-made sign language and that inexplicable understanding that forms when any two people look each other in the eye often enough. This chemistry we shared catapulted her out of the box of "orphan with AIDS" and into her own box. She was just Lakshmi. And I loved her.

It was in this shift of perspective that my trip to India changed my life—which, by the way, isn't the point of mission trips. It's neither to be a saint nor to garner lessons for your own personal growth. Jen Hatmaker expands upon this often-misconstrued "take-away" from these types of trips in her book *For the Love*, which I encourage everyone with a pulse to read as soon as you finish up here. But whether or not it was the point, my life definitely changed. Not because I felt guilty for my privilege. Not because I felt called to "serve more" in volunteerism. But because I was, for the first time, able to see the person behind each persona—even the most distinct or broad, like "orphaned child in India." Lakshmi rocked my life.

When I visited India again two years later at age 18, the men trying to take my bags in the airport were no longer just faces that looked like the ones I'd seen in the documentary when I was in 6th grade. The old lady with leprosy wasn't just a Disney character full of wisdom, sadness, and weathered skin. The kids who'd lost their parents in the 2004 tsunami a few months after my first visit weren't just another batch of third-world orphans.

It spilled over into my life back home.

The girl who intimidated me in my class wasn't just popular and stylish. I wondered what she thought and how she felt. My favorite math teacher probably had a family and a favorite food. Even my mother suddenly seemed more human. *You mean my mom is just a normal person with feelings and interests who just happened to birth me?*

Everyone's story—consciously or not—entered the narrative

of my world. Their intricacies that made them human, unique, and worthy crossed my mind with every interaction. I'm pretty sure this is why I ended up studying psychology in undergrad. I'd always been a pretty empathetic person with an interest in other people, but before India, I lacked the true understanding of humanity comprised of equally worthy and soulful individuals rather than bucketed stereotypes. Finally it clicked—no matter someone's conditions or language or appearance, they hold the same human experience that I do: Worry, fear, joy, embarrassment, hope, love…it's all right there.

A byproduct of both volunteerism and activism is the necessary reminder of shared humanity. This sounds so *basic*. Almost foul in its conclusion. Offensive that I should even type it. But I'm going to remind you (and me) anyway, because basic life lessons tend to be the ones in need of the most TLC:

Humanity lives in all of us.

If you spend your waking hours around only your coworkers, family, and friends (who are most likely very similar to you), then it's all too easy to lose your capacity for deep empathy. Empathy requires considering the experiences of those unlike us. Those who move through life in entirely different circumstances, cultures, and conditions. How easily we stifle our dynamic existence by swimming in the shallow waters of shared experiences.

HOW TO SAVE YOUR OWN LIFE

The New York Times published an article by the Dalai Lama and Arthur C. Brooks in 2016 titled "Behind Our Anxiety: The Fear of Being Unneeded." They wrote that being unneeded is a potentially life-threatening dilemma:

> How strange, then, to see such anger and great discontent in some of the world's richest nations…
>
> …A small hint comes from interesting research about how people thrive. In one shocking experiment, researchers found that senior citizens who didn't feel useful to others were nearly three times as likely to die prematurely as those who did feel useful. This speaks to a broader human truth: We all need to be needed…
>
> …Americans who prioritize doing good for others are almost twice as likely to say they are very happy about their lives…Selflessness and joy are intertwined. The more we are one with the rest of humanity, the better we feel.

Putting forth effort to help other people isn't just about attending protests, spending Saturdays at a nursing home, or writing thank you notes to our troops. Those are, indeed, magnificent ways to spend your time, but at the heart of activism and volunteerism is a lifestyle of service. By lifestyle, I mean that the core values in those undertakings weave their way into your *everyday* life.

You serve your husband by making his favorite oatmeal raisin cookies even though *obviously* the best cookies are chocolate chip. (Please pray mine is eventually imparted wisdom, for I am suffering through too many oatmeal cookies.) You help your neighbor shovel snow off his driveway, drive your friend to the airport, and watch your friend's kids for a few hours so she can grocery shop in peace. You cook a meal for the grieving widow in your church, send your favorite parenting book in the mail to an expecting mom, or foster a puppy from the local shelter.

When service becomes a way of life, you're saving your own.

CHAPTER 8

residence

HOME NOT HOUSE

You know that meme that says "One day you're fun and young, and the next day you wake up and have a favorite spatula"?

I fully get that.

I don't know the actual stats on this, but my guess is that when most of us imagine our futures in middle school, we're not mentally picking out countertops or arranging gallery walls in our heads. We might imagine our wedding dress, our dream job, our sophisticated fashion, or our 30 and flirty and thriving parties, but spatulas? Thread count? Fancy latte machines? Not so much.

Nearly 60% of HGTV viewers are age 30 and older, meaning I'm not alone in valuing home environment much more heavily as I enter the stage in life where stretching before a workout becomes a non-negotiable. Funny, because 18-year-old me really could've used the wisdom of a wholesome Joanna Gaines, but alas, I chose to saturate my pliable mind with lessons from Johnny Bananas. Okay—fine. I still do. I may or may not have hired him to send a personalized video to Aaron on Valentine's Day this year. Best. Present. Ever.

Anyway.

Why would 21-year-olds care about window trim or sectionals when they're busy worrying about what they want to be when they grow up, or falling in love for the first time? I mean, plenty of 30-somethings still face those questions (see: this book), but our coping mechanisms switch from social debauchery to impulse decorating—because, frankly, hangovers are barely worth it anymore.

With the exception of southern sorority house residents, most people begin to take pride in their homes right at that peak moment of *Oh crap am I behind in life??* We want people to think we have our ish together, and where do we keep our ish? At home.

The best way to pretend like you have life figured out other than showering most days is to hang some art and buy a dresser that isn't from IKEA.

Newfound interest in our homes is driven by permanency and ownership—not necessarily becoming homeowners, but committing to one place for a while. You'll know you've entered into this territory when you stop knowing the names of any artists on the radio. Does Billy Eilish scare anyone else? Is Post Malone his given name?

I do want to point out that it's a privilege to even think about what your home looks like or if your name is on the deed. Absolutely. Heck, it's a privilege just to have a roof over your head! Thus, where you live is not a reflection of your truest success, because success isn't tied up in wealth. Success is tied up in *joy*.

With that in mind, if your spic and span 4-bedroom home with white countertops and refurnished hardwood floors is an attempt to advertise that your life is "on track," let me be the first to describe it as a pig with some lipstick on. Remember—there is no track! And using any form of appearance, be it your person or your assets, to bolster your status is missing the point of life: To excel in purpose and in love.

Being rich in your surroundings has nothing to do with money. Slowly step away from the custom Spanish tile. What matters is finding a way to love your *home*, not being concerned about your *house*.

The first step in learning to love where you live? For one thing, take a moment to reflect with gratitude that you have a comfortable place to live at all. And then decide that it's about how *you* feel in your home, not how perfect it looks to other people.

Once you make it about your own taste and sanctuary, you can take it a step further by accepting that no amount of bathrooms or beautifully-arranged open shelving can make you feel satisfied with your life if you don't develop contentment through other, less materialistic means. By all means, design your little heart out, but keep in mind that those walk in closets won't give you a hug when you need it.

Your home is where you recharge, build pillow forts with your kids, and burn turkeys on Thanksgiving. It doesn't have to be big or new or Benjamin Moore Grey Owl. It just has to be home.

OWNING ISN'T WINNING

Do you want to know a term that makes my blood boil? I have a hot temper, so swallow these words if you're near me:

"Starter home."

I know exactly why Scar got so worked up at the single utterance of "Mufasa."

Starter home. *I shudder.* It's almost as bad as mini-moon.

Rant, activated:

Most people save for years before they buy their first house. Maybe it's the only house they'll ever buy! Or maybe someone's buying a smaller home because—gasp—they prefer it! The term "starter home" implies that it's not good enough to be your forever home. That, before you even sign the bottom line, this house is not enough. Because nothing is ever enough. Welcome to America! Prepare to upgrade your white picket fence.

"Starter home" is a ridiculous label intended to keep the real estate business thriving with turnover—a massive form of consumerism. This is all just one more way the world tries to crush your soul by giving unnecessary value to something that won't actually bring you joy.

I'm all about living in a home you absolutely love—so don't get it twisted or interpret this as a dismissal of the importance of your home. No. Not even close. However, the first thing I want to hammer home in this chapter is that you are not behind in life just because you don't have an open floor plan with a double oven. Or because you have to ask a landlord if you have permission to paint the walls.

I didn't write a money chapter of this book because money is tied up in so many of these other subjects—particularly this one. I'm not going to give myself a self-taught degree in the history of finance and subsequently share it here, but I do know that owning a home isn't what it once was. Even if it were, property still doesn't define your worth. It's not going with you when you die, and it's your own dang business why you may choose to rent instead of buy. I've been a homeowner and a renter, and my independence, respectability, and strong money-management skills stayed constant in either scenario.

It doesn't take a wealth manager to realize that with salaries not rising alongside inflation, the higher likelihood of moving cities due to career development, and a whole bunch of other factors I know next to nothing about, owning a home isn't THE answer. Often times you need a *lot* more than the projected five years to break even when you sell if your 1960s plumbing is made out of literal cardboard. You can probably hear the PTSD in my voice.

More people are renting today than at any other point in the last 50 years. If you think you're behind because you don't own a home—think again. Thirty-six percent of households are renting. Heck, my own family and I are renting right now because we're only living in Alaska for three years, on a tiny island where all the homes were built the year the Titanic sunk. We are financially able and shrewd individuals, but for the betterment of our pockets, stress levels, and schedules, someone else can handle the ripped piping in the HVAC.

Do what's best for you! Is aiming to save for an eventual down payment on your own place wise? Sure! Is a savings plan only for people who make a lot of money? Definitely not. It's about managing what you *do* make. But before this becomes a money chapter instead of a housing chapter, may I simply request that you separate any antiquated ideas of success from the beautiful, unique, individual life that belongs to you and only you? Whether you don't own a home because you're a nomad or because you can't afford one in the area you like or you live in a big city where buying is basically impossible—or simply because you forgot to save any of the money you made in your 20s—you are not any less respectable just because you rent the roof over your head.

If homeownership is something you'd like in your future, then do it. Start saving now. Make it happen. You CAN! It's never too late!! But whatever you do, do not let an outdated and arbitrary societal expectation influence your confidence.

In embracing your personal pace and life, the most important ownership you must take is not of real estate. It's of your own decisions.

Make an actual decision, like Aaron and I deciding that renting was our best option while living in Alaska. "Life" didn't make that decision for us. We didn't just fall into it. Enact your educated and thoughtful choice, then remain confident that you're a worthy, admirable, impressive individual no matter what your housing contract looks like. The end.

YOUR HOME MATTERS

Now that we've discussed the irrelevant size and ownership status of your home, let's talk about why the inside of your home does, actually, matter.

There is no better therapy than staring at the snow-capped mountains hovering over a channel of water filled with orcas and charming fishing boats outside the massive 5' x 10' window in our living room. Now, to be clear, a large portion of the population who lives in Ketchikan, Alaska has this exact same view. The entire town is built directly up against the channel where giant cruise ships pile in each summer to get a glimpse of our little oasis.

Real estate up here in The Last Frontier is pretty rad. You almost have to try *not* to have a waterfront view. Where else in the world does the grocery store sit on a postcard worthy backdrop? Is that really in the budget for a building with no windows?? Safeway's café in Ketchikan is what swanky restaurateur dreams are made of. Their breakfast burritos aren't bad either, on the record.

Long story long, I love our view. My toddler might be

throwing uncapped markers at our yappy, skittish four-pound dog while my newborn attempts to rip off my nipples during a midday snack, but I focus my attention on a bald eagle landing in the tree behind our house, and I'm suddenly no longer sweating with mom rage. Sadly, odds are that given my husband's career in the Coast Guard, we won't always live in a secluded rainforest oasis 650 miles from the stress of the lower 48. In fact, we're destined for a life of relocation, so I can't rely on the perfect piece of property to bring me jolts of bald-eagle-level joy whenever I'm sitting on the couch.

Even without the orcas and bald eagles, loving what you see when you walk around your home has more impact on your wellbeing than you might imagine.

The view from a window might be a luxury, but the view of your walls is what you make of it, whether you live in Ketchikan, Alaska or District 12 of Panem. Those of us lucky enough to have a stable roof over our heads are given the opportunity to create an environment that inherently feeds our Best Life mentality.

Our homes are where we start and end the day. Any 10th grade English teacher will tell you that the intro and conclusion are the most memorable and important parts of an essay. They tie everything together, setting the stage and underscoring everything that happens in between.

Your home matters.

Even if you hate HGTV and have no sense of appropriate furniture spacing, Your. Home. Matters.

It does not matter in its size or legal ownership or flooring or location or trendy paint color (though if those things bring you genuine happiness, by all means go ham on your accent wall). What matters is that you make where you start and end your day a reflection of how you want the rest of your life to look:

If you don't want your heart to feel weighty, don't weigh down your home.

If you don't want to feel overwhelmed, don't let your home become overwhelmed.

If you want to be authentic, incorporate your genuine taste into your home.

If you want to live in peaceful gratitude, fill your home with reminders of what you love.

What you see when you start your day sets the tone for your entire day, and either generates joy or dampens your spirit. It's the intro to the essay! But let me, again, repeat myself: This isn't about fancy things or magazine-worthy design.

Is Joanna Gaines an actual goddess walking amongst us? Yes. Is her preference for whitewashed shiplap and subway tile the only measure of residential beauty? No! I happen to love whitewashed shiplap and subway tile, but guess what? I did some major soul searching when we bought our first home, and I realized that gorgeous white everything isn't an honest representation of who I am. I am a colorful person. When I let myself be who I am instead of who I *wish* I was (cough Joanna Gaines cough), I gravitate toward mismatched pillows and floral-meets-metallic gallery walls. Too many frames for some are barely enough for me because I need to see reminders of my loved ones around every corner. Etsy, Hobby Lobby, and I are in a love triangle because personalized dog leash holders and wall décor that says things like "This may be the wine talking, but I love wine" fan the fire of my heart.

When I look around my home, I am happy. Sure, the mountain view is spectacular, but I equally adore the coffee stand with a light up sign that says HANGRY when my husband pushes the button (on my behalf). From the watercolor wallpaper in the nursery to the distressed white wood entertainment stand that I bought off Amazon with old work incentives, each thing I see has intention. That intention inspires a tremendous amount of gratitude that bubbles over into my attitude because I'm just so darn grateful for this little sanctuary we call home. I light up when I spot the faded pink chalk stains on our deck spelling ANDERS and MAMA, or walk past the heavy claw foot dining room table that looks like it belongs in a castle but was actually a hand-me-down from my favorite old boss. It all comprises the best beginning and end I can imagine.

Write your personal story by starting and ending it with joy in your home.

HOW MANY MUFFIN TINS IS TOO MANY?

Stuff. My mom hated it, so now I do, too.

I recently watched an interesting documentary on Netflix about minimalism, which pointed out that the average square footage per home has doubled since the 1950s. This doesn't mean that human beings have suddenly grown into giants—though 5th-graders do look giant these days, and I fear there are too many hormones in their lunchmeat.

So what do we fill our doubly-big homes with if not oversized 5th-graders? *Stuff.*

Essentially, we all pay for fancy storage units. Think about it—you can only eat at one table at a time. That elegant dining room reserved for special occasions goes untouched 363 days a year. Meanwhile, your kitchen table is where nightly memories are made, where you ask how your kid's day was and shoot looks at your husband when you catch him sneaking food to the dog.

My husband believes Joanna Gaines' biggest contribution to society is her disdain for breakfast nooks. She always wants to expand the kitchen into the breakfast nook. It's revolutionary!

Who needs a breakfast nook if you have a dining room table? Maybe I'm not traditional enough for some of you, and that's okay. But Joanna Gaines is onto something.

The unused desk in the home office isn't nearly as convenient as the coffee table, and the spare bedrooms are just glorified closets.

Sure, it's nice to have a room where your cousin can sleep when she's visiting town or a table that's big enough to host Thanksgiving dinner. That's not the issue. The problem is we've come to believe we *need* this extra space. And we feel validated in needing all this space because just look at all the stuff that fills it!

Chicken or the egg?

When Aaron and I were house hunting for our first home, one of the houses I liked (but didn't love) was filled to the brim with proof of children. Toys, gadgets, décor, bins, playsets—the whole nine yards. I don't even want to think about how stressful it was for the owners to keep it organized for showings. During the tour, I asked our real estate agent if he knew why they were moving. It seemed like a great house, after all! He said, "If I had to guess, it's because they're busting out of this place. They clearly need more room."

Immediately I thought, *Do they need more room…or less stuff?*

I'm glad I saw that house before we had kids. I'll never forget it. Aaron and I currently live in a 1500ish square foot home with our toddler and baby. We do not have a playroom, so instead we've arranged a six-cube storage bench beneath the living room window. If toys do not fit in those six bins, they are either carefully vetted for a spot in the rotation, stored neatly in the closet to await their turn, or they go in the donation pile. Thems the rules.

If we had a playroom, I guarantee we'd have one gazillion toys available at all times, of which Anders would play with seven. Because we've been far more intentional about what toys actually bring Anders happiness, all of us have far less crap to deal with. Old toys feel new again with each rotation, saving money and bringing Anders even more joy, since it's like he's reuniting with an old friend each time. If we bring one out of rotation that no longer interests him and isn't worth saving for our second child, then *Poof! Be gone*. Aaron and I are now firmly anti-toy room—at least for our own brand of happiness. The possibility for it to get out of hand and actually detract from Anders' joy is far too likely. Kids can't handle that many choices.

More space and more stuff isn't always a good thing. Don't let the world tell you otherwise. It's not a *bad* thing either—in and of itself—but the point of having stuff and space is to actually use it! For it to improve your life! So if you have 1,000 pictures, but they're all sitting in a drawer somewhere, what is the actual point? Spend a few hours putting them in an album so you can easily flip through them! If you have a sitting room, sit in it! If you have 20 different whisks, you better use all of them or else what are you doing? Mail me a care package with some friggin' cupcakes already.

Remember: When my mom was passing away, she told me to never save the good wine. Don't let it just sit there, waiting for life to be special enough to drink it. Use the good placemats. Display the quilt.

Some say that decluttering is a form of privilege. And to an extent, it is. What if you throw away something that could be of use in the future? Families can't always afford a replacement down the line. I get that. I really do. I know it's hard to get rid of things that bring comfort, or have accumulated in the interest of meeting future needs. What I want for you, for me, for everyone is to free ourselves from the crap that is collecting dust because we've forgotten we even own it.

Aaron and I bought new muffin tins because we didn't realize we had four muffin tins in the garage. I'm trying to save you from the Muffin Tin Catastrophe of 2016! Decluttering isn't about being frivolous. It's about valuing, using, and caring for what you own.

I want us to let go of fear, let go of status, and stare reality in the eye. Are you letting your stuff perpetuate a lifestyle of scarcity, assuming you can't grow or get because your past tells you that's the case? Are you dependent on soulless matter to feed your ego and deprive you of truly fulfilling substance in your life?

This is an exercise in honest personal evaluation, so the outcomes will differ. It's not one size fits all. You're not judging someone else's muffin tins. You're judging your own.

Whenever I find myself getting too attached to material objects or spaces that "would be nice," I remind myself that I cannot bring any of it with me to heaven. I know that sounds pretty lame, like something you might tell your greedy kindergartener when he tries to steal his friend's Easter basket or something. Not that my child would do that. (Just kidding, he definitely would.) But for whatever reason, that campy reminder really works for me.

When I think about my happiness, I do not want it to be tied to things that can burn up in a fire. Yes, I treasure the baby books I've made my kids, and I get really happy when I see the cute produce stand in our kitchen. I'm grateful that I got to decorate a bougie little floral and gold nursery, and honestly love having a bathroom attached to our bedroom. You can unabashedly enjoy material things and spaces (in fact, I'm encouraging you to do exactly that), but when it becomes something greater than a source of gratitude and instead presents itself as a source of status or a crutch, then that environment is no longer serving you. It's suffocating you, snuffing out your ability to focus on the parts of life that actually feed your soul.

Love it? Good.

Attached to its worth or the amount? Bad.

See the difference?

THE 5 TENANTS OF AN ORGANIZED HOME

I don't personally believe in barren walls or chucking your grandmother's good china, but if you look around your home and see a whole bunch of stuff that doesn't have use in your daily life—you're actually risking your own health. Studies have shown that clutter is linked to cortisol levels. As in, you're stressing yourself out by staying attached to a bunch of stuff that doesn't add true value to your life.

That weird little turtle figurine made from ashes of Pompeii that you bought on vacation 12 years ago? Let him go. Send him back out to sea. He'll make friends with Crush—it'll be great! Trust me, Pompeii will still remain, and your vacation will still have happened.

You've got to flex your muscles of discernment and get really honest with yourself about why you have what you have. If you don't have discernment in your home, I'd argue that you lack discernment in other areas of your life, as well. Said it.

Be healthy. Be healthy at home and in your heart and across the whole dang board.

If you're having trouble figuring out what to keep, what to toss, and how to best maintain your home, I highly suggest reading *The Life-Changing Magic of Tidying Up* by the Queen Fairy herself, Marie Kondo. But if this is the only book you ever plan on reading that includes input about the necessity of downsizing your cellophane collection, then feel free to follow the five principles I've compiled that help me wade through my own mess.

1. Everything has a place

If you don't have a designated spot for your 20 scarves other than a folded pile in your closet (which will dissolve as soon as you want the fourth one down), they will soon live in a heap on the floor. I know this from experience. Give everything you own a home—a basket, cubby, drawer, whatever. If you can't find a home for it that's not on the ground, then you have too much stuff.

2. Everything serves a purpose on a regular basis

If you're not using it, wearing it, or enjoying it regularly, then what is it adding to your life? Nothing! Literally nothing, because it just sits there. Doing nothing. I'm not talking about Christmas decorations you bring out once a year or cocktail dresses for wedding season. But if two wedding seasons have passed and you keep ignoring that one dress because you took too many pictures of yourself in it that one time so now its not fun to wear, then do yourself a favor and part ways. Same goes for the bread maker, the fancy lotion someone gifted you four years ago, and the exercise ball mocking you out in the garage.

3. Everything is unique (no unnecessary duplicates)

This one gets to me because my husband loves options. And I love him, bless it. But how many t-shirts does one need? How many ice trays? How many mugs? Not 40, *Aaron.*

4. Everything deserves respect

Do you have to spend 10 minutes finding the lid to your Tupperware each time you make too much spaghetti? Even if your Tupperware follows the first rule and has a home, if it's not kept in a way that makes any sense, then you're not respecting your items. I don't mean this like how Marie Kondo talks to the floor whenever she enters a new space (even though I wish I was that spiritually centered). I just mean that you need to show appreciation for what you have by putting thought into its existence. Is your fridge full of food that's gone bad? Are your plants dying? Are your umbrellas crumpled and twisted? If it's worth having, treat it well.

I really do sound like my mother, wow.

5. Everything is up for evaluation

If you refuse to evaluate the need for something in your home every few years, you've likely crossed over from loving it to being attached to it. Remember that difference we talked about earlier? Check yourself. If you don't want to, check yourself *even harder*.

HOUSE ELVES DO NOT EXIST

One of the biggest areas of feeling like a child in an adult body is the shame that comes with a messy house. This goes beyond the clutter. You're embarrassed that you never graduated into that stage in life where you make your bed every day, or can't bring yourself to do the dishes before the next time you need that cereal bowl. If you've bought new 5 for $25 panties because that's easier than laundry, then you know what I mean. I'm not saying I've done that, but I'm not saying I haven't.

Listen, I'm about to be Mean Mom here for a second, so buckle up. I need you to repeat after me:

If I don't do it, who will?

This is not a rhetorical question, because some of you really believe you have house elves living with you who will literally clean up your mess (i.e. your mother or roommate who resents you). For everyone else, you know for a fact that the old Safeway receipt on your counter will sit there and collect dust until the day you die or move unless you pick up the dang thing and throw it in the trashcan. It's not that hard, people.

If the answer to *If I don't do it, who will?* is "my roommate," we've got to work on your respect and empathy. Do you think your spouse *enjoys* folding your delicates? Do you think your roommate *wants* to wipe down the counters? Don't try to convince me that it makes them happy to take care of you or insist they enjoy cleaning. No one is happy you left your dish in the sink! No one! They take care of it because they value their sanity over leaving it there.

Even if you swear up and down that you don't mind a messy house—get it together, sister. Or mister. Whoever you are. Your home does not need to look like a museum, but pick up that stray sock in the hallway for goodness' sake. Run a vacuum over the carpet so your nasty foot dust doesn't start growing its own toe crust farm in the fibers. Buy a toilet scrubber. They cost like two dollars and require almost no effort if you stow them right behind the bowl.

You'll spend more energy fighting against that inner voice of maturity nagging you than you would just running the vacuum. We've all heard the joke about that one thing you've been putting off for four years taking exactly 15 minutes, and now you realize what a bum you are. Yeah. You are. Do. The. Thing.

I'll tell you why. It's not just because you need to have respect for your housemates or be clean enough to practice spontaneous hospitality. It's not even because it's unhealthy to have mold growing in the back of your fridge or mite-filled bed sheets that haven't been stripped in months—which are all extremely valid reasons, by the way. BUT, none of these are The Reason.

You need to stay on top of housework because of how it will make you feel. Scrubbing counters won't turn you on (or maybe it will, IDK), but when you take consistent little steps to maintain a clean home, you repeatedly give yourself small doses of confidence that add up to something life-changing.

I'm not kidding when I say that quickly shoveling my son's toys back in their bins during naptime is one of the most important parts of my day. Enjoying the train-free floor for two hours is 120 minutes of pure reminder that I am a capable, strong, adult who does mature things like put toys away instead of stepping on them all day and cursing at plastic conductors. I love knowing that I'm giving myself, my husband, and my kids a lower-stress environment. In that, I find more confidence in myself as a mom, wife, and responsible human being.

When I relax in my well kept home with a glass of wine at the end of the day, I feel so much more under control and proud of my life than I was 10 years ago when I slept with my laundry in a heap on the other side of the bed. Come on, singles! Looking at you! You don't have to be a mom to glean some confidence from maintaining your home. Or a woman. Or a clean freak. Every single human alive is wired to gain confidence through actions that remind us we're capable of follow-through. You *must* clean the dish. You *must* throw away junk mail. You *must* use a laundry hamper. You *must*, because I want you to be proud of yourself.

Ed Mylett preaches about confidence being a result of keeping promises you made to yourself, and that is some *truth*, you guys! Do the thing you told yourself you'd do or know you should do! When it's complete, you will feel stronger, more capable, and more worthy. Yes, a glimmering toilet can do all that.

My home isn't whitewashed perfection. I love seeing the baby bouncer in one corner and the lego pad stacked next to the corresponding bin. Our couch pillows are a hodgepodge of TJ Maxx impulse buys and the baby bottles stay next to the sink until my husband gets home to wash them. Washing baby bottles is a pain and he's a saint. But I love my home. Everything in it is intentional. There's even some space in the closets. (Okay, now I'm just bragging.)

CHAPTER 9
faith

LIGHTEN THE LOAD

This topic feels super sticky, no? When I think about discussing faith and religion, I often get the same feeling as watching my toddler run around with syrup fingers—just a general feeling of panic, dread, and wondering which mess I'll have to clean up first. Will it be the atheist I offend because I suggest faith is important at all? Will it be the person who claims all Gods are the same, while I point out that they're not? Or will it be a fellow Christian who focuses on our different biblical interpretations instead of our siblinghood in Jesus?

If I were to focus on those fear-driven questions, though, I probably wouldn't even include this chapter. But I know it's an important one, so let's shake off all the weirdness we carry when it comes to our beliefs in a higher power and give ourselves the freedom to explore spirituality openly, humbly, and without defensive reactions. Isn't this why we often feel behind in this category of life to begin with? We are uncomfortable with opening ourselves up to where faith might lead our lives. We are prideful in thinking it's unnecessary, or that we already know everything we need to know. We are defensive when someone shares a differing belief, assuming that any hint of "right" vs. "wrong" is a hindrance and judgment upon our lives. Thus, religion becomes taboo, awkward, murky, and boxy.

While finding faith and managing the spiritual competition all around us is the focus of this chapter—not my personal faith—I'm going to tell you where I land. I'll get into a bit more detail as to why I landed where I have a bit later, but I'm not going to beat around the bush. In case you haven't gathered this already, I believe in the Christian (aka Christ-driven) God. The one who sent His son to Earth as fully man, yet fully deity (admittedly a difficult concept for our human brains to comprehend), to teach us His ways. His son then undeservedly and willingly died in place of us as a sacrifice so that we won't be held accountable for our sins when we face our eternal fate.

Intense, I know.

Here's the other starting-point caveat, and perhaps the first major sticky-syrup-fingers situation that I'm just going to get out of the way: When I say I believe in the Christian God, I mean that I fully, 100% believe this God exists, that His way is the one true path to salvation, and that I am responsible for living my life as a reaction to this truth. If the God you believe in didn't have a son born to a virgin who died on a cross in order to give humankind the opportunity to have eternal life after death, then we do not believe in the same God.

And we don't have to!

You see, if someone believes something—say, they believe that Velveeta Shells & Cheese is the best mac & cheese there is—then YES, both through implication and direct confession, they do not believe that Kraft Mac & Cheese is the best there is. You simply cannot fully believe two opposing things at the same time. That completely cancels out the word "belief"—to have complete confidence in something's existence. You believe a statement to be true. You believe an ideal to be true. You believe an experience to have happened. Believing isn't wishy-washy. Either you believe or you do not. Can beliefs change? Absolutely! But when they exist—even if eventually altered—they denote a conclusion.

This is something that Western society takes massive issue with these days in the name of tolerance. We are told we are monsters if we believe something that contradicts what someone else believes. Well, *duh*, people! If we believe something and another person believes something else, then yes, they're going to contradict! That's just the way it is!

This is where the defensive reactions come into play. *Well, if they believe in X, and I believe in Y, they are saying that what I believe is wrong. And telling someone they're wrong is just wrong!* Actually, no, it isn't. Treating someone poorly due to differences is wrong. Denying people rights or acceptance is wrong. Thinking you're better or above another person is wrong. But you *can* believe something contradictory to another person while *also* believing that person is worthy of love, respect, friendship, and support. If you want to reference my personal playbook on the matter (the Bible, to be clear), just check out Jesus' behavior toward the woman at the well or his dinner gatherings with the tax collectors. We don't need to walk on eggshells by holding an umbrella over all of our beliefs and insisting that they all must align or else we can't speak of them or be friends.

Let's lay down our swords. We certainly can acknowledge that religion has been the driving force behind some despicable, hateful events, ranging from systemic oppressive movements to private disapproval between family members. However, in order for us to dig deeper into this indescribable pull toward a greater, unseen power that all humans seem to experience, we first must stop seeing religion as the enemy. We've got to let go of the tension we feel when someone mentions a belief that is foreign to us, or contradictory to our own. There has to be a level of humility cloaked in love that allows for the openness required to seek out spiritual fulfillment. If we live in this state of defensive tension, blame, fear, self-righteousness, or tolerance to the point of intolerance, then we'll never reach the place of peace, love, and clarity that our souls ache to find.

Peace and love, man!

Knowing the ins and outs of what you believe, attending particular services, or reaching some enlightened state are not additional rungs on the Ladder of Life. More than anything else—even more than any other subject in this book—spirituality is not measurable or mastered. Even if you land on what you believe when you're young, the way that it infiltrates your life ebs and flows. The ways you learn to apply it to your life grow with maturity and also fail with maturity if we become too rigid.

Faith is ever-changing because our hearts are ever-changing. As the mortals in this duo—not the deity—we are not consistent. Life alters us, and that's going to alter our faith and how we approach it.

Religion. Spirituality. Faith. Whatever you want to call it—it isn't about power or status or checking a box for being a good person. Figuring out what you believe in and *why* is simply a soul's response to a deeper longing. We're looking for answers, purpose, and how to quench this innate thirst to surrender our exhausting control issues. People claim they want complete control of their lives (and the more delusional folk claim to have it), but don't you want a resting place? Somewhere to lay your burdens? I, for one, don't have the strength to rely on myself or other faulty humans to get through this life.

Whether you know exactly where your spiritual beliefs lie, or you haven't given it much thought because it all seems a bit too mystifying and controversial, I can guarantee a massive life-improvement if you let faith become central to your existence. Not so that you can look good or hold profound conversation, but to lighten your load and live with wholehearted connection, purpose, and unwavering security.

SPIRITUAL GROWTH

Based solely on my observations of friends, colleagues, and random people I follow on social media, the sweeping trust in what we were taught to believe seems to take a nosedive sometime in young adulthood. People who grew up in super religious or legalistic homes begin to wonder if there's more freedom in a life without parameters. Those who came from families who never spoke of a higher power begin to wonder if there's something out there they've yet to discover.

This is a good thing. The only true path to genuine belief in a spiritual guide and creator is to take ownership of what's in your mind. In other words, you *must* question your inherited beliefs.

Personally, I have never lost the steadfast tug on my heart that says *God is real*, no matter what stage of life I've found myself. I want that for my kids. I pray for it, because that certainty is a gift. The thing is, though—I had to figure out what that unwavering tug *meant* to me. For me. About me.

For my fellow knowers, we must take ownership of our *why* and *how*, even if the *what* has always been clear.

In figuring out *why* we believe what we do and *how* that will impact the decisions we make and the perspectives we hold, we further solidify the *what*. For example, my *what* is that I believe in the Christian God, and the more I've dug into *why* I believe that (by reading books, taking note of experiences in my life, conversing with others, and examining my heart) and *how* that reflects in my life (I choose to not judge, not self-loathe, read my Bible and pray every day, and be part of a fellowship of like-minded believers), the more I feel confident about my *what*. God is real. He is good.

When I was young(er), my faith was more easily shaken because I didn't own my *why* and *how*. I was told the *why* was because I should be afraid of hell, and that my *how* was to alienate myself from people different from me and silently condemn them in a self-righteous-cloaked-in-concern manner. Once I broke free from that narrative, I still had my *what*, but it became about five million percent stronger once I did some digging to form my own *why* and *how*.

Maybe your *what* isn't as clear. Maybe the tug on your heart tells you that you've got the wrong *what* altogether. Maybe what you believe in—be it an organized religion or even the absence of religion—doesn't sit well with your soul. Good. This is a breakthrough.

One of my mentors calls that negative-tug—that not-sitting-well feeling—"tension." She said it's that same feeling you get when you think about the pair of jeans in your drawer that no longer fit you. If you get that same tense feeling when it comes to your *what*, it's time to dig.

The same can apply to your *why* and *how*, by the way. If *how* your beliefs infiltrate your life creates tension in your heart (ex: "Wait, does it actually reflect Jesus to degrade another human being?"), then it's time to make some changes there, as well.

What does all of this *who what where why how* mumbo jumbo mean, exactly? It means you have your starting point!

Starting Point #1: If you are sure of your *what*, your starting point is to develop your *why* and *how*.

I realized around age 19 that "because my parents told me" was no longer a decent *why*. It's just not a good look. It was time to buckle up and do my own research, evaluate my own life, and let that exploration lead me to a well-built foundation of faith.

Going through life ignoring that ache to be part of something bigger—denying yourself a peace that can't be shaken—is a terrible trade off for being unwilling to part with an hour of Netflix to research. We've all got to put a little work into honing the spiritual depths of our souls.

Be intentional in identifying clear, specific reasons *why* you believe (or don't) what you do. A big one for me when I start questioning my faith was to remember my experience with God when my mom died. I'll share more about my story here in a few pages, but that specific event is my cornerstone. Yes, I know Jesus is *the* cornerstone. It's in the Bible *and* a popular worship song! Double zing! But the foundation of my faith can't be shaken when I remember that my *why* lies in those hours before and after my mother's passing. It helps identify my *what* when it becomes blurry.

And then there's the *how*. Believing in something isn't enough. I know that's not a popular school of thought, but I've never been popular and neither were Jesus' disciples, so I'm in good company. How your faith affects your choices is the truest indicator of what you believe.

It's the same concept as saying you love someone, but you continually ignore them. How does that make any sense? If you love someone, your actions line up. If you believe in something or someone—truly, actually believe, not just a make-believe hokey thing in your head—then your actions will align.

I asked my mom some hard questions as she was dying. One of them was, "What if God isn't real?" She said, "Well, loving others, not gossiping, not worrying about tomorrow, not getting caught up in complicated lustful relationships—it was still the best way to live."

Starting Point #2: Find your *what*.

For those of you who question the entire shebang, your journey goes beyond the *why* and *how*. You must open yourself up to a whole new world. A new fantastic point of view.

The easiest way to start this journey is by listening. Ask your friends what they believe, and listen to their answers. Maybe watch a few YouTube videos with people sharing basic principles of their faith. YouTube has everything! It is your friend! (It is also very scary.) If you've accidentally found yourself only surrounded by like-minded individuals, that is no longer an excuse to be out of touch with alternate viewpoints.

Listen and see what resonates with you.

Try praying.

Try scripture.

Try it all!

When I was in college, I ended up one class short of a minor in religious studies because I decided to use my elective courses to study religions that were different from the one I was taught. Like I mentioned, I always had this tug on my heart that knew God—the Christian God—was the Truth, but I had recently been burned by His church, and decided I wanted to revisit my *what* completely.

The first class I took was Religions of the East, followed by Religions of the West the next semester. Then I signed up for a course on Buddhism, as well as one about spirituality as it relates to psychology. In digesting all of this information, learning what, exactly, people around the world believe and how it has impacted history, culture, and communities, I not only gained a broader understanding of our world, but ultimately, I became more grounded in my own beliefs. You see, exploration is a *necessity*.

MY STORY

Christianity has been the most directly influential part of my life, but I rarely spoke about it until the last few years. Why? Because my journey has been unconventional, extreme, painful, negative, and at points, embarrassing. It has also been positive, lifesaving, comforting, and uplifting. I hadn't wanted to speak of what I'd been through because much of it revolves around mistreatment and poor leadership from the church in which I was raised. Talking about what happened in that church doesn't sit well with me because I in no way think that the large majority of members harbor poor intentions, controlling tendencies, or mean spirits. When reading this, please bear in mind that my objective is not to blanket an entire congregation. I also don't want my story to reflect poorly on God, in whom I fully believe and trust.

Legalism seeps into organized religion because churches are made up of people, and people are inherently sinful. We mess up. We are not perfect. We easily become prideful, hypocritical, and selfish. For Christians, this is the whole reason Jesus existed—to nullify the unavoidable sins of human nature. Why are we surprised that churches make mistakes and at times hurt their members? After all, a church is nothing more than a body of individuals—and no individual, even a church leader, is exempt from poor choices.

I grew up in a nondenominational church my mother joined in 1991. The church was an international, evangelical movement with radical practices to ensure that its members followed the Bible's commandments. What started as the honest objective to separate themselves from "Sunday Christians" deteriorated into a loss of grace and love. Instead, deeds and rules became the focus. Many of the members wanted nothing more than to love God and humbly live for Him, but a culture of accusatory accountability, harsh rebukes, and guilt-driven requirements led to the suppression of those good intentions.

I went to church on Sundays and Wednesdays, Bible Talk on Mondays, and devotionals on Fridays. I met with my discipler (a person older in the faith assigned for accountability and mentorship) once a week. I participated in prayer groups, bible studies, quiet times and everything in between. If I befriended anyone outside of the church, I was told that I was being sinful unless I convinced them to join our church. Dating was to be only within the church, given permission from leaders. I had a dress code that included t-shirts and shorts at the beach, was constantly hounded to confess things that I did not necessarily feel or do, and felt pressured to alienate myself from anyone not within the church.

These constraints and expectations were intended to keep us away from temptation, but only fueled people-pleasing rather than God-pleasing tendencies. I wanted so badly to delight God—sincerely—and was trained to do so by adhering to mandates of church leaders.

My mother never succumbed to raising me with a controlling hand, so none of these rules were of her making. My father was not part of the church, so naturally he did not enforce (or support) the legalism either. Eventually, my mom chose to leave the church a few years after my parents divorced in order to marry my stepdad—a man of extraordinary faith who the church did not permit my mom to marry since he was not baptized under their surveillance.

Breaking ties with a particular organization did not shake my mom's faith, but my brother and I continued to attend since neither of us wanted to lose the world in which we lived and found comfort. After all, we distinctly separated ourselves from "the world" (non-members, even ones who claimed to be Christians), so leaving the church would mean finding ourselves in unfamiliar, vast territory. My mother did not want that anxiety placed on us, knowing that the fragile teenage psyche could be easily devastated if rejected by the only community it's ever known. Thus, she let us forge our own spiritual paths with God and this church, trusting Him in a way I never appreciated until years and years later.

My older brother left the church after his first year in college. A rising senior in high school, I was told over and over how "strong" I was for being the only one in my family "left." People who leave church are called "fall-aways"—and I was surrounded by them.

Toward the end of my senior year, I remember telling my discipler that I wanted to move to New York City to pursue musical theatre, but was met with disapproval since my career passion was "too self-indulgent." Mind you, a brilliant friend of mine in the church at the time wanted to go to medical school, but was told to pursue a less demanding academic track so that he could be trained for church leadership instead. Anything that was not about the church was considered wrong. Following the advice of church leaders, I accepted my admission to a small liberal arts school near my hometown and focused on how I could best serve God through the campus ministry.

The summer before my freshman year at Christopher Newport University (Go Captains! No regrets—I love my alma mater!), in the midst of a rebuke for something I had done wrong (admittedly…after all, I was 18 and human), for the first time, I felt a twinge of *Wait…is this actually how I should be treated right now?* The woman verbally punishing me for my sin asked, "What do you think about all of this?" when she finished her spiel. I earnestly replied, "I know that you're telling me this out of love, and I just want to repent." I meant it. I vividly remember her huffing, "You know what, Shannon? I don't even know if I'm doing this out of love. But I'm doing it because it's right."

Wait, what?

I chalked my initial offense at this statement up to the fact that I was being prideful. I had sinned, so who was I to focus on someone else—particularly my spiritual "superior"—wronging me?

Despite other small instances of unease nagging the back of my mind (ex: being told not to sing my prayers as I enjoyed doing because that relied too much on loving the sound of my own voice…here I was thinking I was given my voice to praise Him…?), I dove headfirst into freshman year like it was a conversion excursion.

Then I met David.

Ruh roh! He's cute.

I invited him to church and he became a member (score!), but we secretly started dating since the church did not approve our relationship (he was "too young of a Christian"). The lying and deceit to keep our relationship under wraps only spiraled into more and more sin until I couldn't take the double life any longer. Just when we were on the brink of being exposed (my best friend knew what was going on), he and I confessed to everything.

It escalated quickly.

First, we were instructed to have no contact whatsoever until the church decided how they would handle the situation. In David's case, they called into question whether or not his conversion was legitimate. For me, they had to decide if I would be "disfellowshipped" (excommunicated from the church) since this was not my first offense. For two weeks following our confession, I met with leaders to be rebuked, questioned, and challenged. Leadership decided to tell the entire church body of my transgressions, based on Matthew 18:15:

> [15] *"If your brother or sister sins, go and point out their fault, just between the two of you. If they listen to you, you have won them over. 16 But if they will not listen, take one or two others along, so that 'every matter may be established by the testimony of two or three witnesses.' 17 If they still refuse to listen, tell it to the church; and if they refuse to listen even to the church, treat them as you would a pagan or a tax collector."*

When reading that scripture, keep in mind that I still wanted to live for God and most definitely was listening to the church. But I'll skip the interpretation dilemma for the sake of word count.

I sat in front of everyone I knew as the leader behind the pulpit called me out by name and said that I'd been "immoral." Immoral = had sex. Me in the audience = virgin. I forced my faith to cushion the blow, deciding it didn't matter since only God was important. I needed to be humbled in front of the church. This was good for me.

A few days later, I sat in a room in the student union and listened to a leader tell me over and over how stupid I was. "Shannon, you're just stupid! You don't lie and have a secret relationship unless you're stupid. It's one of the stupidest things anyone can do. You are stupid!" Super productive language. Among the countless meetings, only two or three people showed me any love or compassion.

Three weeks after the initial confession and plenty more cases of harsh—erm—"guidance," David texted me simply to say that he was having a hard time. I didn't know what he had been experiencing in those three weeks, but I figured if it was anything close to what I had, he must be pretty low. Without thinking, I responded, "I'm really sorry." After I pressed send, it hit me that I'd have to lie about sending that text if I didn't want to be disfellowshipped. The whole point of confessing was because I didn't want to lie anymore. I had one of two choices: Leave by force or leave on my own.

I wrote a letter to my roommate (a church member, of course, because living with anyone in the world would be bad bad bad) and to the campus leader, then left town for the weekend, not wanting to be around for the reaction. I received emails and voicemails saying, *We know you're with David. What is wrong with you??* along with an array other choice words. When I returned to campus on Sunday night, my roommate had moved out since she could no longer associate with me. A fall-away. I'd known her since I was eight.

Over the next few days, the only people I had ever been close to in life defriended me on Facebook. I later found out that a random married man in the church who I barely knew had messaged everyone on Facebook telling them to cut me off. Why did he care so much? Honestly, as I look back, it kind of creeps me out.

On top of losing all of my friends, I was scared of God. For nearly a year, I was convinced that a mailbox next to me would explode and I'd die and go to hell. I thought that God hated me for leaving "His church." I believed everything the church had taught me about fall-aways—and now I was one of them. Unlike many people who leave this church, I did not lose faith in God. I believed in Him. I just thought I was going to suffer eternally.

The members of the church sure didn't help that notion. Ten days after I left, 32 students were killed in the Virginia Tech massacre. My ex-discipler—a campus leader and pastor's daughter—texted me to say that it could have been at CNU, it could have been me, and I would have gone to hell. I was terrified.

My boyfriend and I stayed together for about two years after leaving the church. I joined a sorority and an all-female a cappella group in order to develop new friendships. The women I met in those organizations showed me more unconditional love than I'd been taught in the 15 years I attended the church. I could trust that they weren't talking about me behind my back under the pretense of "how Shannon is doing spiritually," I knew they'd love me even if I left their organizations, and they fully forgave me for all of the things I did wrong. Which was and is a *lot*. Never claimed I was a saint!

Time went on and I became less fearful, but I also bottled up a lot of my turmoil surrounding how I'd ever feel loved by God again. I chose not to think about Him because I figured my demise in hell was inevitable unless I returned to the church—and I simply did not plan to do that. Here and there, people popped up in my life that inspired me to accept God as loving and forgiving rather than narrowly jealous and wrathful, but I couldn't fully get past the fact that these Christians did not belong to THE church...were they just watered-down and emotional followers? I grew up never trusting anyone's faith outside of the church, so grasping outsiders' hearts for God was far from easy.

After six years of no involvement with any sort of fellowship, my mother's battle with cancer brought God right back to the forefront of my mind. Her faith during her five-month ordeal was extraordinary. No one in the room with her during those last few weeks could deny God's existence. Even my family members who were agnostic or atheist started believing in God because of the Holy Spirit that surrounded her. Awe-inspiring does not begin to cover it.

Though my faith had never completely disappeared, I could no longer live without addressing it. When I held my mom's hand as she passed away, my first thought was that she was meeting God at that very moment. How could that kind of comfort be ignored?

Over the next few years, I redeveloped my relationship with God. It did not happen overnight, but I knew I believed in God, would strive to live within His will, and trusted in the sacrifice of Jesus to cover over my multitude of sins. Mul. Ti. Tude. That's for sure. I settled into knowing that I do not (and should not) take advantage of His sacrifice, but in accepting my need for it, I understood its magnitude more than ever before. I accepted that my deeds are not what save me—it's Jesus and my faith in Him. Yes, my deeds should reflect my faith as the book of James outlines, but that does not mean that I'll never give into temptation or that I need to self-loathe if I do.

I am grateful for my time in "the church." In it, I developed the foundation for my faith, learned the scriptures, stayed out of way more trouble as a teenager than had I been "normal," and made amazing memories with people I still care deeply about. Most importantly, I absolutely know that my involvement was for the greater good of my relationship with God, and that is something I can and will never regret.

A quick snapshot of my life now: God is the center of my life, my family, and my purpose. I have friends who are both believers and non-believers, and I love them all equally. I love singing—mostly to my babies—and drinking wine. Lots of wine. (Again, Jesus turning water to wine is my favorite miracle.)

Guilt sometimes threatens to plague me, but with each day that I pray for God to remind me of His love and grace, that guilt turns into pure gratitude.

All in all, I'm happy—a recipient of the deep, soulful joy that we're all looking for. This happiness isn't because I give into doing whatever I feel like in the moment; rather, it exists because everything in life has led me to a place where

I get to lean on a perfect, loving, and forgiving God who will never leave me or forsake me. And as my mom said in her final hours, He is good. All the time.

AROUND THE DINNER TABLE

I can't stand the saying that you should never discuss politics or religion at the dinner table. I'm all for a communal psychological dissection of the cast of *Love is Blind* (Jessica Messica sharing her wine glass with her dog is a whole mood), but at some point we need to reignite the power of civil discourse. This idea that we can't separate religion from emotional judgment and frustration is a cop-out and an insult to reason. By taking the subject off the table, we've basically been told it's okay—nay, inevitable—to go down a judgy, defensive, aggressive path whenever we talk about religion. *Don't talk about it at all*, they say, *because there is no other option besides dissention.*

Sit down! There is *for sure* another option! We are entirely in control of how we speak, respond, and interpret. We abso*lute*ly hold that power!

The way you interact with other human beings is a decision. No matter the emotion you feel in reaction to opposition—perhaps fear, sadness, anger, embarrassment, confusion, frustration—you get to *choose* how that emotion manifests in your words, tone, and behavior. Is it always easy? No! That's because our beliefs—remember, what we *know* to be true, 100%—require passion in order to exist. To be passionate is to be emotional, and that emotion desperately wants to spill over into how and what we say. That's not necessarily a bad thing.

I tell you what, if you try to tell me that pineapple belongs on pizza, I will passionately react with disgust because I believe—I *know*—that you are wrong. So so wrong.

Respecting our own passion, therefore emotions, while maintaining our composure is a skill. I can't just dramatically feed the pineapple pizza to the dog in a fit of disgust and showiness. (I mean, *I have*, but that doesn't mean it was the best choice.)

The ability to behave with a level head does not lessen your resolve or mean you're willing to sideline your convictions. In fact—quite the opposite! How often do you ponder a different perspective if it's being yelled into your ears? Or if it's shared in a condescending Facebook post? Probably never. Those tactics are cringey and upsetting. But if someone shares from a passionate, educated, and vulnerable place, it's more likely to give you pause. This goes both ways! We give life to our own beliefs by communicating in a manner that elicits thoughtful engagement, and our composure puts us in a more open headspace to gain new perspective as we listen. Rationally sharing and discussing our beliefs with someone is like a having a convictions workout buddy!

You know what I want? I want the guilt-tripping, manhandling, gang-up mentality to get gone. *Go now, git!* I am tired of complicated human beings being labeled Good or Bad as if we can be fully either. I want religious people to worship God, not political parties. I just want the anger to stop. I want the love to begin. The active, hard core, do-something-about-it kind of love that doesn't blanket an entire group of individuals or insist upon black and white doctrine when there is, in fact, a whole lot of grey.

How, though? How do you talk about your faith and face its challengers head-on without getting worked up? How do you do it without seeming pretentious, thus compromising your reach? How do you avoid fragility and unproductive yammering? How do you stand up for a belief if you can't prove it, or perhaps know there's some loophole you've yet to iron out?

I have some practical ground rules that I think you'll find very helpful. At least, they've helped me. I hope this list will change your Thanksgiving dinners, change your relationships, and change your life. Because when we figure out how to speak freely about who we are and what we believe, we're no longer trapped inside that swirly tornado of pent up dread, and instead can lean into the integrity of our souls. It feels so good.

Oh, just a note—these six bullets build off of one another, so they're intertwined as much as they're independent.

1. Go into the conversation fully prepared to not change any minds

If you find yourself in a discussion about religion where you know there are differing viewpoints—be it entirely different belief systems, or different convictions, practices, or traditions under the same umbrella—then before you open your mouth, before you engage, before you even breathe, take a sip of wine. Kidding. Or not. But seriously, before you engage, the very first thing you must consciously, intentionally, and assertively remind yourself is that they will not change their mind based on what you say.

You might be able to cause them to ponder a few things in the shower that night, but in almost zero circumstances will someone wrap up a conversation with you by saying, "I've been completely wrong all this time, so thank you for showing me the light."

We get annoyed or self-righteous because *we just can't understand how they don't get it.* Bad news—they think the same thing about you. If you have an opinion and someone else has a different one, everyone in the room has their own reasoning.

So your intent in engaging cannot be to change someone's mind. Certainly not in one sitting.

I remember once reading about an atheist who said he finds no fault in evangelical Christians, for if they truly believe Jesus' teachings to be true, then he'd be offended if they didn't try to save him from hell. That's just common courtesy! I wish I could find this author's exact words, because I love them so. (Please let me know if you have any idea what or who I'm talking about.) You see, it's not necessarily a bad thing to want to bring someone under your umbrella. In fact, it only makes sense that you want to help people find the same joy or salvation you have. That's a form of love!

However, there's a fine line between caring and controlling. If you think someone should and will change their mind because of your own eloquent debate skills or oh-so-righteous demeanor, then you'll never get the results you want. In fact, you're pridefully relying on yourself instead of trusting in God's power to incite change without your measly little intervention. That's super counteractive to your whole mission! Unimpressive! We must remove our fragile egos from the conversation and be comfortable with ending the discourse without resolution. This has nothing to do with not caring enough or being an inadequate representative, but instead makes room for actual spiritual growth for both parties. (Yes, that means you!) The end goal of being "right" can actually suffocate any budding stimulation toward a converging path.

Catch this: You can be expressing yourself in a convincing manner without expectation to convince. In religious discussions, there is no winner. So be like Elsa, and let it go.

2. Whatever you do, do not condescend

Just because you know what you believe does not mean that you know everything. When we're passionately defending our case and bringing new perspective or information to the table, it's all too easy to talk down as though we're teaching something obvious. You know the phrase "Don't talk to me like a child"? Well that's because when we talk to our kids, we're teaching them very basic, rudimentary skills or expectations. *No, Benny,*

2 + 2 is FOUR! Adults have developed brains that are capable of putting two and two together. Making someone feel stupid is not only pointless, but it's a poor reflection of your own communication skills.

3. Approach your points with vulnerable, first-hand reasoning

Okay, if condescension and a winner-takes-all mentality don't work, what does?

Make it personal.

The best way to engage your audience in a way that doesn't offend, attack, or degrade is by demolishing your own walls.

I had an old boss that used to say that anyone who believes in God is dimwitted. I used to want to say, "Well, then why did you hire me? Only a dimwit would hire a dimwit!" BURN.

But I didn't.

One time, I simply said, "Well, I believe in God," and he gave me a funny look, then walked away. Hey, it was something! But what I wish I'd done is tell him why. He was smarter than me, older than me, and potentially had a greater volume of rationalizations to support his beliefs (or lack there of)—but sometimes I wish I'd had the courage to say, "I believe in God because not only does history support the prophetic teachings found on scrolls written thousands of years before the outcomes took place *(whew that would've been a mouthful)*, but also because when my mother died, some truly undeniable, faith-building encounters took place. It's something you may not be able to understand unless you were in the room when she died like I was."

Is that going to suddenly make this man a believer? Probably not. But will he be offended or angry? No. Instead, a response like that would've made room for him to comprehend that perhaps my beliefs are from a place of knowledge and experience outside his sphere of thinking. Plus he'd feel like a real jerkface.

4. Find common ground

In productively discussing opposing beliefs, interpretations, or convictions, there are no words more powerful than "I agree." Not, "I agree, but…"—no, just "I agree." Period. By validating something your adversary says without rebuttal, not only do you set the tone for respect by giving it to them, but you garner that same respect because they'll think, *Oh, well this person isn't a total lunatic if they agree with me!*

Thus, you've created space for them to digest other contributions you make, rather than just plan their own defense as you speak. Finding even one area of common ground (or however many you can!) is a tremendous force to catapult the conversation into the realm of fruitful discourse.

5. Be confident while not having all the answers

One of the biggest myths of all time is that admitting you don't know something is proof of your inadequacy.

The only time this is the case is in customer service. Lord be with the representative who tells me they don't know the answer to something instead of saying, "Let me find that out for you." Blood boiler.

Your argument isn't weakened if you admit you don't have a good answer. It doesn't mean you have to concede your convictions (unless you should), but there's no harm in saying, "I completely see why you think that way, and I don't have a good answer for my side of things. I'm looking forward to digging into that a bit more."

Boom! All done! You look reasonable and the argument is over. Isn't that nice?

6. Be entirely wary of the internet

Social media isn't going anywhere, so keyboard debates are going to be part of our world whether we like it or not. But I have one question for you: Can you think of a single instance that a heated online debate produced anything good? I don't mean online social justice movements. I mean comment threads with everything from quick, biting comebacks, to wildly sweeping generalizations, to meticulous arguments meant to outsmart their opponents with more formal knowledge, vocabulary, and life experience. Oh man, those smarty-pants arguments kill me.

I understand how tempting it is to "call someone out," but isn't the point of challenging someone to actually incite change? If you truly believe they are missing something or spreading a harmful message, why wouldn't you approach them in a manner that has a legitimate chance of reaching their hearts instead of provoking their fight or flight?

Not that everyone always needs to hear your opinion, anyway.

Still, there's a way to do things that causes further division, and there's a way to do things that actually works. If you must engage online instead of in person, all of the rules prior to this one are applicable. Do so with vulnerability and humility, find common ground, don't condescend, and be consciously aware that changing someone's mind isn't a one comment or one conversation journey. Standing up for what you believe is honorable, but doing so in a way that contradicts love or strips the possibility of further conversation that can induce true growth—well, that's a real waste of convictions. We must keep the humanity in our voices online, because cancel culture and hate—specifically in the realm of beliefs that aren't actively hurting someone—do not have a place in any worthy belief system.

And while we're on the subject of the interwebs, do us all a favor and fact check.

Check your beliefs. Check your heart. And check out the last section of this book, because it's next! You did it! Proud of you for reading. Sometimes it's hard when Netflix has all 16 seasons of *Grey's Anatomy*.

final thoughts

I kind of can't believe I'm writing the conclusion to my book. Am I allowed to say that? Is that not formal enough? But I'm inappropriately excited because this entire book is a testament to all of the words inside of it.

That's a bit meta. Let me explain.

I've always felt behind in life. If this surprises you, then I hate to be the one to break the news that any author who is an expert on a subject is so because that topic was the root of some sort of struggle in their life. For me, one of the centerpieces of my "by now" mindset was this nagging feeling that as a longtime blogger and, ahem, Features Editor of my high school newspaper (I don't want to talk about why I wasn't Editor-in-Chief...big dreams die hard, even 14 years later), I should have written a book *by now*. I felt like this big ole loser full of potential that never made its way to the surface.

Well, it turns out that I'm not dead! (Except in the moments I am clutching a pint of Half Baked ice cream, staring blankly at an episode of *New Girl* after my child screams for 30 straight minutes before bed.) My "timeline" still had plenty of wiggle room. I could still write the book. So I did.

Would I have been able to write a book from a place of such deep personal connection and experience had I written this when I was 24? Probably not. Though if a 24-year-old wants to write a book, I highly recommend it. You're a freaking rock star and I am so glad you're living your best life instead of falling asleep on the New York City subway in the middle of the night and waking up in Coney Island like in my 24th year of life. They were the best of times, they were the worst of times.

Each of us is thriving in at least one area of a traditional timely sense, which I'm sure you gathered as you flipped these pages. You may have happily tied the knot at age 21, so the relationship chapter was just a friendly reminder of the hellhole called dating that you escaped unsinged. Or maybe you've always had a cute home, a fulfilling career, or 2.5 kids who self potty-trained. *I will not roll my eyes, I will not roll my eyes, I will not roll my eyes.*

But no one has it all. Not a one. "By now" makes zero sense. Your life is your LIFE! It is linear only in sunrises and sunsets, not in the makeup of each of rotation. Plus, veering "off track" can be fun! You'll write better books! Find bigger love!

Once you stop viewing your life as what it should be and start seeing it for the unique presence it actually is, that's when things get exciting. That's when you sit down at eight months pregnant and start busting out your first chapter. That's when you start learning what a roux is and how to make it. That's when you sign a lease on a whim and meet the love of your life. When you see your life as a pliable piece of living art, you realize that it's never too late or too unconventional to form the joy and confidence you're looking for.

Sure, you can't make someone to fall in love with you (ask any Disney witch) or be guaranteed to become a mega pop star instead of an insurance agent, but you *can* take intentional steps to open yourself up to those possibilities. Remember, in everything, control what you can, and let the rest do its thing!

In giving yourself the leeway to live a life that is fully, deeply, unapologetically your own, the burden of the passing time lifts from your shoulders. The light bulb pops on and you can see that your story is a beaut! Maybe a little rough around the edges, but she's a real beaut.

It's time to cultivate that beauty and activate joy.

I want you to live in a home you love, be it 250 square feet (shout out to my Washington Heights studio!) or 10,000 square feet. I want you to know your worth whether you're single or married. I want you to fall in love with not just a person, but the right person. I want you to not loathe your job or be defined by money. I want you to connect with the needs of others so your joy can be fueled by shared humanity and gratitude. I want you to pray to a God you know and love by choice and encounter. I want your children to be complicated, sticky little humans, not prize-winning farm animals, and your tragedies to be part of your story but not the ending.

I want all of this for you. And the greatest part is knowing that it's entirely possible. My hope for your lives and mine to be vibrant and appreciated (by you, yourself!) is alive and well because you are alive, too. You are the youiest you've ever been, even if you've been partially zapped into your screens or slapped sideways by misfortune.

Your missed opportunities, your potential, your greatest accomplishments, your failures, your dreams—they all live under one roof. The roof! The roof! The roof is on fire! Except it's not. Your life is still in the works—still yours for the taking. It always has been, and always will be.

So while you take life in your hands and drop it, then pick it back up and drop it again, try not to worry. You're completely normal.

acknowledgments

I always read the thank you sections of books. It's one of my favorite parts—to see all the names of the people who champion the author while I giggle at inside jokes I know nothing about and feel all the feels about supportive relationships. I also imagine who I'd write about. Whose names mean so much to me.

So the first recipient in my very own thank you section is you. You, Reader. For reading not just the book, but this particular section. For understanding that this book is more than just a helpful compilation of words that was encouraging or entertaining. This book is an actual dream come true. In your very hands! *Someone's dream!* Mine, to be exact. And I thank you for realizing that this dream wouldn't exist without the names you're about to read. Something tells me that people who read acknowledgements are people with dreams, too. People who have names in mind for their own thank you list. Love them well, for it is an honor to forever tie their names to yours!

Kathleen Hibbets. Mom. Thank you for telling me not to save the good wine. Thank you for raising me to take action.

To make it happen. I wish you were here to read this, but I have no doubt that you still guide me so closely that your heart is on these pages, too.

Aaron Leyko. My love. My fortress and my free fall. With you I am protected, strong, and able, while equally vulnerable, raw, and needy as heck. (Sorry for being such a pain.) That combination is why this book exists. Your belief in me is the greatest blessing of my lifetime. You believed I would write this. (And write it well!) You believe I am a wonderful mother, wife, daughter, sister, friend, leader, creator, cook (how did this happen??), and follower of Christ. It's your belief that keeps me going when I falter. Thank you for making me your Number 1. I needed you. My mom knew I did. I still can't believe you're real.

Anderson and Josephine Leyko. Noma Noodle Leyko, too. One day when you're old enough to read this, I hope you know that you inspired me to leave a legacy with my words—to achieve a dream so that one day you will reach for yours, as well. Thank you for being such wonderful nappers so I could write these words before you woke up and demanded *Dinosaur Train* (Anders) and mama milk (Jo). Noma, you'll never be able to read, but thanks for being so soft.

J.D. Oliver, Jean MacLeay (Oliver if only the DMV wasn't such a pain), Drew Oliver, Jim Oliver, Lindsay Oliver, and Papa Ronald MacLeay. You love me unconditionally and put up with me in my 20s so that Chapter 1 of this book could exist. You deserve all the wine. I love you.

Sherwin Hibbets, Becky Hibbets, Aunt Leslie Harrington,

Grandma Lois Baker, Jill "Jilly Bean" Baldauf, Dianna Ackerly, Sharon Taylor, and everyone who preserves the memory of my mom. You love me well and continue to give me strength as her daughter to accomplish my goals.

Katlyn Wilson, Madison Embrey, Emily Herman, Caroline Bright, and Molly Carter. My dream team. Thank you for editing this book that barely made an iota of sense when I sent it to you. Thank you for sending me your favorite parts as you were reading so that I'd stop sweating profusely at the thought of your returned manuscripts that I was sure would each be one giant red X. Thank you for kindly telling me when my words were offensive or irrelevant or boring. You were so lavishly gentle in your delivery that I occasionally laughed out loud at the truly eloquent ways you came up with to tell me something sucked. I don't deserve any of you. I love you, and thank you.

Mrs. Susan Buchanan. Thank you for teaching me how to write and making me believe in my gift.

Mrs. Joan Kennedy. You always saw talent in me beyond my singing, and I'm certain I wouldn't have the confidence to write a book without years of using our voice lessons as weekly therapy sessions.

Annie Hutton. Your wisdom and faith sticks with me to this day. Thank you for those too-few months of mentorship before I moved to Virginia Beach. My relationship with God and all that comes from it—including this book—would not be what it is without you. I also pray that someday I can be half as funny as you are.

Randy Singer. You sharpen my faith and inspire me both spiritually and professionally. I'll be forever grateful you reached out to me when my mom was sick. Your pastoral leadership is extraordinary. Also, thank you for being willing to counsel Aaron and me (alongside Rhonda) before our whirlwind wedding and serve as our officiant. So far, so good!

Melina Glover. You take the most exquisite photos. Thanks for doing the cover shoot for this book so last minute and for your patience with my rowdy family who always turns your studio into a carnival.

Vanessa Booth. I didn't even know you don't do custom orders when I asked you to make the hat for the cover of this book, but not only did you say "yes," you made TWO options!! I'm so grateful we met that one fateful night on my first visit to Alaska. You're a gem. I wish you lots of sunshine and travel.

Vanessa Mendozzi. Thank you for designing a book so beautiful that my family and friends saw the cover and said things like, "Oh my gosh, it looks like a *real* book!" I fear that without you, people might've thought this elusive "book" I was writing said things like "asasdgkasdgskssss" or "ydao-idgjjsjjjddd" on the inside.

My friends. I'd name all of you but that would be ridiculous. You know who you are. Some of us grew up together, some of us worked together, some of us went to college together or did pageants together or are raising our babies with one another on speed dial because *what do I do with these crazy children???* You are my people. You guys know I love a deep conversation but you also accept that I'm cheesy and weird and like shallow escapes like *The Bachelor* or Top 40 music. You're the reason I apparently have a memorable writing voice. Throughout the years, you've let me be *me*. Thank you for such extraordinary acceptance and love.

Last, because my roots are tied in robotic pageant speeches but also because I mean it, I want to thank God. He exists and He is good. Thank you for answered prayers—the yeses and the nos—that continue to work for the good of Your Kingdom. Thank you for the purpose, the peace, and the passion. Thank you for instilling faith in my heart so I can have all three. Those gifts live on these pages.

NOTES

CHAPTER 1

"Marital Status & Poverty," Social Security Administration, 2016, https://www.ssa.gov/policy/docs/population-profiles/marital-status-poverty.html.

"Maybe our girlfriends are our soulmates and guys are just people to have fun with." Candace Bushnell, *Sex and the City* (New York: Warner Books, 1997).

Paul Gray, "What is Love," time.com, June 21, 2001, http://content.time.com/time/magazine/article/0,9171,161039,00.html.

Frank Newport and Joy Wilke, "Most in the U.S. Want Marriage, but Its Importance Has Dropped," gallup.com, August 2, 2013, https://news.gallup.com/poll/163802/marriage-importance-dropped.aspx.

Wendy Wange and Kim Parker, "Chapter 1: Public Views on Marriage," Pew Research Center, Social & Demographic Trends, pewresearch.org, September 24, 2014, https://www.pewsocialtrends.org/2014/09/24/chapter-1-public-views-on-marriage/.

"What Do Americans Think of Marriage?" 60 Minutes/Vanity Fair, January 26, 2017, https://www.vanityfair.com/culture/2017/01/what-do-americans-think-of-marriage.

https://www.neverlikeditanyway.com.

Shel Silverstein, "Masks," *Everything On It* (New York: HarperCollins, 2011).

Marriage Report 2017, bridebook.co.uk, https://bridebook.co.uk/article/bridebook-co-uk-marriage-report-2017.

Ted L. Huston, Sylvia Niehuis, and Shanna E. Smith. "Courtship and the Newlywed Years: What They Tell Us About the Future of a Marriage", (1994), http://app.cubender.com/downloads/80792/documents/56courtship_and_the_newlywed_years_what_they_tell_us_about_the_future_of_a_marriage_2000.pdf (Accessed September 16, 2020).

Aziz Ansari, *Modern Romance*, Penguin Books (2016), bbc.com, https://www.bbc.com/news/magazine-35535424.

Michael Rosenfeld, *Disintermediating your friends: How online dating in the United States displaces other ways of meeting (2019)*, Proceedings of the National Academy of Sciences of the United States of America, https://www.pnas.org/content/116/36/17753 (Accessed September 16, 2020).

Andy Stanley, *The New Rules for Love, Sex, and Dating*, Grand Rapids: Zondervan (2016).

Seth Stephens-Davidowitz, *Everybody Lies: Big Data, New Data, and What the Internet Can Tell Us About Who We Really Are*, New York: Dey Street Books (2017), 122, 160.

The Bible, *New International Version.* 1 Corinthians 6.16, Biblica (2011), *BibleGateway.com, https://www.biblegateway.com/passage/?search=1%20Corinthians%206%3A16&version=NIV.*

Robert J. Davis, *How Exercise Can Improve Your Sex Life*, health.com, June 2, 2017, https://www.health.com/sex/exercise-and-sex.

Kyle Benson, *The Magic Relationship Ratio, According to Science*, The Gottman Institute, October 4, 2017, https://www.gottman.com/blog/the-magic-relationship-ratio-according-science/.

J.K. Rowling, *Harry Potter and the Philosopher's Stone*. New York: Arthur A. Levine Books (1997).

Jane E. Brody, *When a Partner Cheats*, nytimes.com, January 22, 2018, https://www.nytimes.com/2018/01/22/well/marriage-cheating-infidelity.html.

CHAPTER TWO

Lydia Saad, "The '40-Hour' Workweek is Actually Longer -- by Seven Hours," news.gallup.com, August 29, 2014, https://news.gallup.com/poll/175286/hour-workweek-actually-longer-seven-hours.aspx.

Jeffrey M. Jones, "In U.S., 40% Get Less Than Recommended Amount of Sleep," news.gallup.com, December 19, 2013, https://news.gallup.com/poll/166553/less-recommended-amount-sleep.aspx.

The Conference Board, "Labor Day Survey: 51% of U.S. Employees Overall Satisfied with Their Job," prnewswire.com, August 29, 2018, https://www.prnewswire.com/news-releases/labor-day-survey-51-of-us-employees-overall-satisfied-with-their-job-300704255.html.

Henry Ford, "Whether you believe you can do a thing or not, you are right." *The Reader's Digest*, September 1947.

Marcus Buckingham, "What Great Managers Do," Harvard Business Review, March 2015, https://hbr.org/2005/03/what-great-managers-do.

Jon Christiansen, "8 Things Leaders Do That Make Employees Quit," Harvard Business Review, September 10, 2019, https://hbr.org/2019/09/8-things-leaders-do-that-make-employees-quit.

Greg McKeown, *Essentialism: The Disciplined Pursuit of Less*, (New York; Crown Business, 2014).

Jaison R. Abel and Richard Deitz, "Do Big Cities Help College Graduates Find Better Jobs?", Federal Reserve Bank of

New York, Liberty Street Economics, May 20, 2013, https://libertystreeteconomics.newyorkfed.org/2013/05/do-big-cities-help-college-graduates-find-better-jobs.html.

Lou Adler, "New Survey Reveals 85% of All Jobs are Filled Via Networking," linkedin.com, February 29, 2016, https://www.linkedin.com/pulse/new-survey-reveals-85-all-jobs-filled-via-networking-lou-adler.

CHAPTER 3

Trevor Haynes, "Dopamine, Smartphones, & You: A battle for your time," *Science In the News*, harvard.edu, May 1, 2018, http://sitn.hms.harvard.edu/flash/2018/dopamine-smartphones-battle-time/.

Hayley C. Cuccinello, "Instagram Star Essena O'Neill Quits Social Media, Exposes the Business Behind Her Pics," forbes.com, November 3, 2015, https://www.forbes.com/sites/hayleycuccinello/2015/11/03/instagram-star-essena-oneill-quits-social-media-exposes-the-business-behind-her-pics/#5a9707392ad5.

Jonah Engel Bromwich, "Essena O'Neill, Instagram Star, Recaptions Her Life," nytimes.com, November 3, 2015, https://www.nytimes.com/2015/11/04/fashion/essena-oneill-instagram-star-recaptions-her-life.html.

Kerry Chan-Laddaran, "Instagram Star Essena O'Neill: Social Media is Not Real," cnn.com, November 4, 2015, https://www.cnn.com/2015/11/03/entertainment/social-media-essena-oneill-irpt/index.html

Kate Fagan, "Split Image," espn.com, May 7, 2015, http://www.espn.com/espn/feature/story/_/id/12833146/instagram-account-university-pennsylvania-runner-showed-only-part-story.

David Ludden Ph.D., "Does Using Social Media Make you Lonely?" psychologytoday.com, January 24, 2018, https://www.psychologytoday.com/us/blog/talking-apes/201801/

does-using-social-media-make-you-lonely.

"How Much Time Do People Spend on Social Media," Industry Report (2019), saasscout.com, https://saasscout.com/time-spent-on-social-media/.

"Nine Themes of Digital Citizenship," digitalcitizenship.net (2017), https://www.digitalcitizenship.net/nine-elements.html.

CHAPTER 4

David Garner, "Body Image in America: Survey Results," Psychology Today, September 14, 2017, https://www.psychologytoday.com/us/articles/199702/body-image-in-america-survey-results.

Tina Fey, *Bossypants* (New York: Little, Brown and Co, 2011).

"Obesity and Overweight," cdc.gov, National Center for Health Statistics (2015-2016), https://www.cdc.gov/nchs/fastats/obesity-overweight.htm.

"U.S. Weight Loss Market Worth $66 Billion," prnewswire.com, December 20, 2017, https://www.prnewswire.com/news-releases/us-weight-loss-market-worth-66-billion-300573968.html.

"23 Exceptional Fad Diet Statistics," healthresearchfunding.org, https://healthresearchfunding.org/23-exceptional-fad-diet-statistics/.

Gillian Zoe Segal, "Warren Buffett wants young people to know: Ignoring this is like 'leaving a car out in hailstorms,'" cnbc.com, April 15, 2019, https://www.cnbc.com/2019/04/12/billionaire-warren-buffett-greatest-advice-to-millennials-the-1-thing-in-life-you-need-to-prioritize.html.

John J. Ratey MD, Spark: The Revolutionary New Science of Exercise and the Brain (New York: Little, Brown Spark, 2008).

Kristen Stewart, "How Exercise Works Like a Drug for ADHD," everydayhealth.com, December 16, 2013, https://www.everydayhealth.com/add-adhd/can-you-exercise-away-adhd-symptoms.aspx.

Jamie Ducharme, "About 90% of Americans Don't Eat Enough Fruits and Vegetables," time.com, November 17, 2017, https://www.everydayhealth.com/add-adhd/can-you-exercise-away-adhd-symptoms.aspx.

"Timex Survey Reveals Nation's Exercise Habits," Timex Group, prnewswire.com, September 11, 2013, https://www.prnewswire.com/news-releases/timex-survey-reveals-nations-exercise-habits-223279731.html.

Christina Gough, "Total number of memberships at fitness centers/health clubs in the U.S. from 2000 to 2017," statista.com, July 3, 2019, https://www.statista.com/statistics/236123/us-fitness-center--health-club-memberships/.

CHAPTER 5

Richard F. Taflinger, "Social Basis of Human Behavior: Sex," wsu.edu, May 28, 1996, https://public.wsu.edu/~taflinge/socsex.html.

Alyson J. Lumley and Lukasz Michalczyk, *Sexual Selection Protects Against Extinction*, Macmillan Publishers Limited, 2015, nature.com (accessed October 20, 2020), https://www.nature.com/articles/nature14419.

"Miscarriage: What is it?" Harvard Health Publishing, Harvard Medical School, health.harvard.edu, February 2019, https://www.health.harvard.edu/a_to_z/miscarriage-a-to-z.

Adoption Disruption and Dissolution, childwelfare.gov, June 2012, https://www.childwelfare.gov/pubPDFs/s_disrup.pdf.

“Key Statistics for Childhood Cancers,” cancer.org, August 24, 2020, https://www.cancer.org/cancer/cancer-in-children/key-statistics.html.

“Almost 800 Kids Drown Each Year; More than Half are Under Age 5,” safekids.org, June 29, 2016, https://www.safekids.org/press-release/almost-800-kids-drown-each-year-more-half-are-under-age-5.

“About SUID and SIDS,” cdc.gov, April 29, 2020, https://www.cdc.gov/sids/about/index.htm?CDC_AA_refVal=https%3A%2F%2Fwww.cdc.gov%2Fsids%2FAboutSUIDandSIDS.htm.

“Understanding the Incidence of Sudden Unexplained Death in Child (SUDC),” SUDC Foundation, sudc.org, https://sudc.org/understanding-the-incidence-of-sudden-unexplained-death-in-child-sudc/.

Elizabeth Stone, Quotes, goodreads.com, https://www.goodreads.com/quotes/14913-making-the-decision-to-have-a-child---it-is.

Stephanie Kramer, “U.S. Has World’s Highest Rate of Children Living in Single-Parent Households,” pewresearch.org, December 12, 2019, https://www.pewresearch.org/fact-tank/2019/12/12/u-s-children-more-likely-than-children-in-other-countries-to-live-with-just-one-parent/.

“The State of LD: Understanding the 1 in 5,” National Center for Learning Disabilities, ncld.org, May 2, 2017, https://ncld.org/news/newsroom/the-state-of-ld-understanding-the-1-in-5.

Birth Defects, cdc.gov, August 5, 2020, https://www.cdc.gov/ncbddd/birthdefects/index.html.

Major Depression, National Institute of Mental Health, nimh.nih.gov, February 2019, https://www.nimh.nih.gov/health/statistics/major-depression.shtml.

Jenna Carberg and Kimberly Langdon M.D., "Postpartum Depression Statistics," postpartumdepression.org, May 3, 2019, https://www.postpartumdepression.org/resources/statistics/.

Nicholas H. Wolfinger, "Does Having Children Make People Happier in the Long Run?" Institute for Family Studies, ifstudies.org, December 10, 2018, https://ifstudies.org/blog/does-having-children-make-people-happier-in-the-long-run.

CHAPTER 6

Bill Murray, Quotes, https://www.azquotes.com/quote/879380.

Michael F. Steger and Todd B. Kashdan, "Depression and Everyday Social Activity, Belonging, and Well-Being," National Center for Biotechnology Information, ncbi.nlm.nih.gov, April 27, 2010, https://www.ncbi.nlm.nih.gov/pmc/articles/PMC2860146/.

Tasha Cain, "Study Says the Average American Hasn't Made a New Friend in Half a Decade," wtsp.com, May 12, 2019, https://www.wtsp.com/article/life/study-says-the-average-american-hasnt-made-a-new-friend-in-half-a-decade/67-61e09c92-ab6d-4d82-a505-056604aa76d9.

"What Percentage of Americans Currently Live in the Town or City Where They Grew Up?" northamerican.com, 2016, https://www.northamerican.com/infographics/where-they-grew-up.

Stephanie Pappas, "7 Ways Friendships Are Great for Your Health," livescience.com, January 8, 2016, https://www.livescience.com/53315-how-friendships-are-good-for-your-health.html.

CHAPTER 7

Jeff Boss, "How to Overcome The 'Analysis Paralysis' of Decision-Making," forbes.com, May 20, 2015, https://www.forbes.com/sites/jeffboss/2015/03/20/how-to-overcome-the-analysis-paralysis-of-decision-making/#6d4a59c01be5.

Miss Americana, Directed by Lana Wilson, performance by Taylor Swift, Tremolo Productions, 2020. *Netflix*, https://www.netflix.com/title/81028336.

Alison Lynch, "'I would like to be excluded from this narrative' is the perfect response to any awkward situation," metro.co.uk, July 29, 2016, https://metro.co.uk/2016/07/19/i-would-like-to-be-excluded-from-this-narrative-is-your-new-favourite-get-out-6015031/.

Neil Postman, *Amusing Ourselves to Death: Public Discourse in the Age of Show Business,* New York: Penguin Books, 1986.

Kathryn Lorenz MD, "Screen Addiction Affects Physical and Mental Health," premierhealth.com, December 5, 2019, https://www.premierhealth.com/your-health/articles/health-topics/screen-addiction-affects-physical-and-mental-health

"Not a single person asked me how fast I could run in my new shoes today. Being an adult is...stupid," @cptnman, Tweet.

Peter Gray Ph.D, "The Decline of Play and Rise in Children's Mental Disorders," psychologytoday.com, January 26, 2010, https://www.psychologytoday.com/us/blog/freedom-learn/201001/the-decline-play-and-rise-in-childrens-mental-disorders.

Julian Rotter, "Internal Versus External Control of Reinforcement: A Case History of a Variable," *American Psychologist*, April 1990, 490-493.

Bonnie Rochman, "Yay for Recess: Pediatricians Say It's as Important as Math or Reading," time.com, December 31, 2012, https://healthland.time.com/2012/12/31/yay-for-recess-pediatricians-say-its-as-important-as-math-or-reading/.

Jen Hatmaker. *For the Love.* Nashville: Thomas Nelson, 2018.

Dalai Lama and Arthur C. Brooks, "Behind Our Anxiety: The Fear of Being Unneeded," nytimes.com, November 4, 2016, https://www.nytimes.com/2016/11/04/opinion/

dalai-lama-behind-our-anxiety-the-fear-of-being-unneeded.html.

CHAPTER 8

Statista Research Department, "Share of Americans who watched HGTV in the past month in 2018, by age," statista.com, January 21, 2020, https://www.statista.com/statistics/228962/cable-tv-networks-hgtv-watched-in-the-last-7-days-usa/.

Anthony Cilluffo, A.W. Geiger, and Richard Fry, "More U.S. households are renting than at any point in 50 years," pewresearch.org, July 19, 2017, https://www.pewresearch.org/fact-tank/2017/07/19/more-u-s-households-are-renting-than-at-any-point-in-50-years/.

Suzanne Collins. *Hunger Games*. New York: Scholastic, 2008.

Minimalism: A Documentary About the Important Things, Directed by Matt D'Avella, performance by Joshua Fields Millburn and Ryan Nicodemus, 2016. *Netflix*, https://www.netflix.com/title/80114460.

"Behind the Ever-Expanding American Dream House", *All Things Considered*, NPR, July 4, 2006, https://www.npr.org/templates/story/story.php?storyId=5525283.

Emilie Le Beau Lucchesi, "The Unbearable Heaviness of Clutter," nytimes.com, January 3, 2019, https://www.nytimes.com/2019/01/03/well/mind/clutter-stress-procrastination-psychology.html.

Marie Kondo, *The Life-Changing Magic of Tidying Up: The Japanese Art of Decluttering and Organizing*. First American edition. Berkeley: Ten Speed Press, 2014.

Ed Mylett, Facebook @EdMylettFanPage, March 28, 2019, https://www.facebook.com/watch/?v=385425355373001&extid=LLumj9JC6PSf3mtJ.

CHAPTER 9

The Bible, *New International Version*. Matthew 18:15, Biblica (2011), *BibleGateway.com,* https://www.biblegateway.com/passage/?search=Matthew%2018:15&version=NIV.

Philip R. Davies, "Dead Sea Scrolls," britannica.com, September 14, 2020, https://www.britannica.com/topic/Dead-Sea-Scrolls.

Dr. Seuss, *Happy Birthday to You!*, New York: Random House Children's Books, 1959.

Rock Master Scott & the Dynamic Three, "The Roof is On Fire," 1984.

Made in the USA
Middletown, DE
23 November 2020

24951732R00224